# MYSTERY AND MIME
# IN THE RIG VEDA

## INDRA, THE MARUTS, AND AGASTYA

LEOPOLD VON SCHROEDER

*Translated by*
ALEXANDER JACOB

*Mystery and Mime in the Rig Veda: Indra, the Maruts, and Agastya*
Leopold von Schroeder
Translated by Alexander Jacob

978-0-6486072-7-4

Thema Classification: QRD (Hinduism), QRDF1 (Hindu Texts), 1QBA (Ancient History).

MANTICORE PRESS
WWW.MANTICORE.PRESS

# CONTENTS

# INTRODUCTION

ALEXANDER JACO3

Leopold von Schroeder (1851-1920) was born in Dorpat (Tartu) in Estonia and began his studies in Comparative Linguistics at the University of Dorpat in 1870. After further studies at the Universities of Leipzig, Jena, and Tübingen, he obtained his master's degree in Indology from the University of Dorpat in 1877. From 1882 Schroeder was employed as a lecturer in Indology at the University of Dorpat. In 1896 he was appointed professor of Indology at the University of Innsbruck in Austria and, from1899, at the University of Vienna.

Schroeder made significant contributions to the understanding of Indo-European mythology in works such as *Griechische Götter und Heroen* (1887) and *Germanische Elben und Götter beim Estenvolke* (1906) and also published several Indological and comparative mythological studies focused on ancient Indian literature. These include *Ueber die Mâitrâyani Samhita* (1879), *Pythagoras und die Inder* (1884), *Buddhismus und Christenthum* (1893), *Mysterium und Mimus im Rigveda* (1908), *Bhagavad-gita, des Erhabenen Sang*

(1912), *Herakles und Indra* (1914) and *Arische Religion* (2 vols., 1914-1916).

Schroeder's close friendship with Houston Stewart Chamberlain (1855-1927) brought him into contact with the circle of Richard Wagner and he contributed several articles to the *Bayreuther Blätter*. He also wrote a major study of Wagner's music dramas, *Die Vollendung des arischen Mysteriums in Bayreuth* (1910), which was an elaborate exercise in comparative Indo-European mythology.

Schroeder's study of the mimetic aspects of the Rig Veda, *Mysterium und Mimus im Rigveda*, includes seventeen chapters devoted to texts that are not typical of sacrificial liturgies. Of these the first chapter discusses the texts of *RV* I,170,171 and 165. Schroeder believed that the dialogue sections of these Rigvedic hymns reflected an earlier dramatic version of these hymns that was lost when the Vedic hymns were transformed into purely liturgical texts.

Schroeder, in his Introduction to the work, adduces as supports for his theory the example of a few Vedic hymns that seem to have no basis in ritual practice such as the lament of a dice player who has lost all his money through his game, the song of a doctor who extols the merits of his pharmacy, and the song about frogs that are compared to priests and students.[1] As regards the dialogue hymns in the Vedas, Hermann Oldenberg had suggested that there may have existed a special type of literature, Ākhyāna, that included verses supplemented by prose texts. Sylvain Lévi and Johannes Hertel, on

---

[1]   See *Mysterium und Mimus*, 'Einleitung'.

the other hand, had advanced the theory that these dialogue hymns, especially in the *Sāma Veda*, indeed represented an early form of dramatic art among the Vedic peoples that included actions, declamations, choral songs, and dances. This led Schroeder to connect this supposed early form of Indic drama with the dramatic representations of Crete, Greece, Italy, and the Germanic lands and especially with the sacred dances and sword dances developed therefrom. The songs of the *Edda* in particular, Schroeder reminds us, are characterized by a large number of dialogues.

Schroeder believed that such dramatic representations were part of the earliest mystery cults that preceded the sacrificial worship of the Āryans.[2] The latter excluded drama and sometimes even opposed it, when it contained phallic ceremonies, such as those celebrated in the ancient Mediterranean. Schroeder laments the loss of the mystery aspect of religious cult in the Vedic period:

> The priestly ritualists of the Vedic age let much of folkloric nature that originated from the earliest times be stylized in a sacral manner and ossified: racing and discus-throwing, igniting and brandishing fire, and much more. And other things of this sort they let completely disappear. And among these is also clearly the religious drama, the mystery – perhaps the most severe loss in this sense, at any rate that which is most to be lamented by us.

---

[2] We know from Aristotle's *Poetics* 1449a that Greek tragedy developed from the spoken preludes to the Dionysian dithyrambs. But, as we shall see later, it is doubtful that these Dionysian mysteries were entirely Āryan in origin.

However, these dramatic aspects of a presumed earlier mystery cult were preserved in later mediaeval times in the religious dramas based on the Shiva and Vishnu cults of India.

Schroeder's theory may indeed support the idea suggested by F.E. Pargiter that Brāhmanism itself was not originally Āryan but adopted into Indo-Āryan religion from non-Āryan peoples.[3] We may remember also that in the *Bhāgavata Purāna* (VIII,14,3) the First Man, Manu, is called Satyavrata, King of Dravida. *BP* VIII,24,13 informs us further that the role of a 'Manu' is to maintain the cosmic order at the time of the creation of the universe. So we may assume that Dravida and its king Satyavrata represent the first fully enlightened, and religious, mankind. And from the Biblical evidence we notice that Noah, the Hebrew equivalent of Manu, has three sons, Ham, Shem, and Japheth, who represent the Hamites, the Semites, and the Indo-Europeans respectively. It is possible that the mystery cults postulated by Schroeder in the earliest history of the Āryans were cultic practices of the Hamitic peoples, as exhibited, for example, in the dance of the Curetes and Corybantes, who – as we shall see – are not of Āryan origin but rather of Hamitic.

It may be noted, in this context, that the Āryans designated the Dasyus or non-Āryans as Anagni, the fireless.[4] The reference in *Manusmrithi* X:43-45 to "the Dravidas, the Kāmbojas [Persians], the Yavanas [Ionians], the Sakas [Scythians], etc." as Kshatriya races

---

[3] See F.E. Pargiter, *Ancieni Indian Historical Tradition*, London: Milford. 1922. Ch.26.

[4] See P.T. Srinivasa Iyengar's 1927 lectures at the University of Madras, *Pre-Aryan Tamil Culture*, New Delhi: Asian Educational Services, 1985, p.2.

which have sunk to the level of Shūdras on account of their neglect of the sacred rites and the authority of the Brāhmans suggests that Brāhmanism, though based on the spiritual insights of the proto-Dravidians and mostly magical in character, was, after the entry of the Indo-Āryans into India, formulated as an exclusively fire-worshipping cult.[5] The cosmological insights that informed later Brāhmanism may, however, have been obtained through Yogic discipline by a pre-Āryan people and absorbed by the Āryans in the course of their diverse migrations.

Schroeder's effort to understand these hymns as relics of an earlier Āryan drama related to the mysteries thus ignores the distinctive quality of fire-worship among the earliest Āryans and the possibility of the origin of mystery cults among Hamitic, rather than Japhetic, peoples. However, while Schroeder's thesis may not be very fruitful in the study of Vedic ritual, his focus on the primal mystery cults may help to illuminate the birth of the dramatic arts both in ancient Europe and in the India of the *Nātya Shāstra*[6] in the early centuries B.C.

---

[5]  According to *Rāmāyana,* Uttarakanda, 100, Ila was the son of the Manu Kardama, and king of Bāhlika (Bactria). Pururavas, a grandson of Chandra and Ila, acquired the sacred fires of the Āryans from the Gandharvas. The archaeological evidence of the early Gandharvas may be that found in the Gandhara Grave culture of the Swat settled from 1700-1400 B.C. following the Bactro-Margiana Archaeological Complex (ca.220-1700 B.C.).

[6]  The *Nātya Shāstra* is the standard Indian treatise on the dramatic arts composed in the early centuries B.C. According to this text (I,17), however, Brahma invented drama by combining recitation from the *Rig Veda,* singing from the *Sāma Veda,* mime from the *Yajur Veda* and the expression of sentiments from the *Atharva Veda.*

In the first chapter of the present work Schroeder attempts to demonstrate his thesis by discussing three chapters of the first book of the *Rig Veda*, where a dialogue is presented between Indra, the Maruts, and the sage Agastya[7] regarding a sacrifice that is to be presented by the latter. Agastya had originally intended to offer the sacrifice to the Maruts but Indra, who is their superior, is enraged by the apparent slight to his own eminence as a warrior and demands that he be acknowledged as the sole vanquisher of the dragon Vrtra, whose defeat releases the solar rays that had been allowed to congeal in the underworld.

In *RV* I,170 the Maruts are sorely disappointed at the estrangement that has developed between them and Indra and the resulting lack of a sacrifice to them. In *RV* I,171, Agastya explains that he had aborted the sacrifice to them on account of his fear of Indra's mighty wrath and hopes for a reconciliation between the two parties. In *RV* I,165, Indra replies to the Maruts' inquiries regarding his unusual aloofness by declaring that he had indeed been abandoned by the Maruts in his fight against Vrtra. At this, the Maruts hasten to reassert their devotion to Indra, remind him of their previous assistance to him and promise him their continued support in the future. This reassurance seems to please Indra and Agastya then proceeds to offer the sacrifice to the Maruts that he had previously curtailed.

There is little evidence that the three scenes that Schroeder discusses actually formed part of a play. Indeed, most of the Rigvedic hymns are not dramatic in

---

[7]    Agastya is the author of the Rig Vedic hymns I,165-191. He is one of the Seven Sages of Vedic lore and the one who brought Vedic knowledge to South India, where he is revered as the author of the first Tamil grammar called *Agattiyam*.

structure but invocations of various deities that attempt to ensure their attendance at the sacrifice that is being prepared for them and to make sure that they partake of the offerings. This participation will strengthen the deities and, at the same time, ensure the success of the sacrificer in his various desires, for wealth, health, or progeny.

It should also be noted that Schroeder's presentation of the diffusion of the Rig Vedic myth of Indra and the Maruts among the related Indo-European peoples, such as the Italic and Germanic peoples, generally ignores the cosmic dimension of Āryan mythology. Thus the tremendous cosmic forces represented by Indra and the Maruts are mostly understood as 'storm gods' and 'rain gods.' The birth of the sun also constitutes the climactic act of the cosmic drama and is represented as the mere birth of a new year. While this reduction of cosmic phenomena to atmospheric ones may have occurred in the course of time even in India, it is important not to lose sight of the cosmological basis of all Indo-European mythologies. To this end it may be useful to briefly repeat here the reconstruction of ancient Indo-European cosmogony that I first presented in my study *Ātman: A Reconstruction of the Solar Cosmology of the Indo-Europeans.*[8]

At the end of the first cosmic age, the supreme Soul (**Ātman**/Shiva), desirous of creation, acquires through the fervour (**Agni**) of his desire an ideal macroanthropomorphic form as the **Purusha.** From the nostrils of this macroanthropos emerges the life-breath

---

[8]  See A. Jacob, *Ātman: A Reconstruction of the Solar Cosmology of the Indo-Europeans,* Hildesheim: Georg Olms, 2005.

of the deity, Vāyu,[9] in the form of a Boar[10] which recovers the Earth sunk at the bottom of the cosmic ocean during the flood that brought the first cosmic age to a close. The boar/Vāyu then impregnates and spreads Earth, producing, as a result, extended Earth (Prithvi/Gaia) and its "cover" primal Heaven (Brahman/(Dyaus/Ouranos) in a closely united complex.

However, the temporal concomitant of the rapidly moving Wind-form of the supreme deity, Shiva/Kāla/**Chronos**, separates the united Heaven and Earth by castrating the Purusha, since the phallus is the instrument of desire as well as of life. The semen that falls from the castrated phallus of Heaven impregnates the Purusha bound to Earth with a Cosmic Egg, from which then emerges the **manifest cosmos** constituted of Earth, in the form of a lotus, crowned with a Heaven of divine Light and Consciousness (Brahman/Helios). The ruler of this primal cosmos is Chronos.

This manifest Purusha, or macroanthropos, crowned with effulgent Light (Brahman/Ouranos) is, however, shattered by the persistent stormy aspect (or 'son') of Chronos – Zeus/Indra/Ganesha – and forced to descend into the nether regions of the "lotus"

---

[9]  The Germanic Wotan must be identified with the Indo-Iranian Wāta, a companion of Vāyu, the god of 'Wind' (the source of Prāna/life-breath). While Wāta is not a clearly defined deity in the Vedas, he is – in the Middle Persian version of Zoroastrianism called Zurvanism (from 'Zurvan', Time) – represented as a companion of Vāyu, and denotes the spatial aspect of the original life-breath or air. Thus, while Vāyu represents the life-breath, Wāta is space. In the Avesta's 'Ram Yasht', the chief deity worshipped is Vāyu, who is described as the one who 'goes through the two worlds, Heaven and Earth' of our universe.

[10]  In the Indic *Bhāgavata Purāna*, the boar is the second, early cosmic, incarnation of the supreme deity (called Vishnu, his solar form) and, in the Avestan Yasht 14, the first form of Verethragna (corresponding to the Indic Vishnu and Indra) is Wāta, and the fifth form is as a boar.

Earth. Zeus/Ganesha, however, preserves the castrated phallus of the ideal Man (containing the life of our yet unmanifested universe) by swallowing it.[11]

In the underworld, where the Purusha lies moribund as the Lord of Earth (Skt. Varuna/Ir. Xvarenah/It. Quirinus) surrounded by an Ocean (Okeanos), the stormy and vital aspect of the same force (Zeus/Indra/Thor) destroys the serpent of material resistance (Vrtra/Typhon) that surrounds the Earth and divides its body into the heaven and earth of **our universe.** Imbibing the aphrodisiac juice 'Soma,' which is the essence of the desire that caused Dyaus/ Ouranos/Heaven to mate with Earth in the primal cosmos, Indra/Wotan/Dionysus then rejuvenates the Lord of Earth and the divine phallus, which then rises – between heaven and earth – in the mid-region of the stars as our universe.

The entire universe informed by the life-giving force of Soma is now shaped in the form of a "Tree of Life" (Ashvatta/Indra), an analogue of the divine phallus itself, whose roots are in the underworld, trunk and branches in the mid-region, and its peak in heaven. The chthonic elements of this Tree of Life, however,

---

[11] The commentator of the Orphic Derveni theogony explains that Zeus indeed swallowed "the sexual organ" [aidion] (see M.L. West, *Orphic Poems*, p.85). In other versions of the Orphic theogony, Phanes 'counterpart of Brahman) is said to be devoured by Zeus (see M.L. West, *op.cit.*, p88f.) thereby absorbing the original universe into himself, but we may assume that it is the phallus of Phanes that is thus consumed. In the *Shiva Pūrana*, Ganesha, like his counterparts Zeus/Indra, is said to have attacked Brahma – just as his father Shiva/Kāla attacked the primal Heaven of the Purusha. Ganesha is depicted with an elephant's head bearing a phallic trunk and with a "pot-belly" which contains the entire universe (see S.L. Nagar, *The Cult of Vinayaka*, N.Delhi: Intellectual Publishing House, 1992, p.115).

have to be purified, and this is accomplished by the self-sacrifice of the wind-god (Vāyu/Iranian Wāta/Wotan) on the universal tree.[12] This done, the seed of the phallus bearing the life and light of the original Cosmic Man is finally free to emerge in our universe as the **sun**.

We see, therefore, that there are two distinct stages in the evolution of our cosmos, the first marked by the formation of the ideal, macroanthropomorphic Purusha, being the primal cosmos ruled by the Titan Chronos, and the second marked by the rise of our universe from the sunken Heaven, Dyaus, in the nether regions of Earth.[13] This universe is ruled by the god Zeus/Indra. The divine forces that rule in our universe are related to those that ruled the original cosmos even though their operations and effects are rather different.

**Indra** is indeed the principal god of the Vedic Indo-Āryans and the one most often invoked in the Rig Veda. His exploits in the underworld – where he imbibes the life-force of Soma, destroys the serpent of resistance Vrtra, and releases the solar energy and the waters of the seven rivers of the universe – are described in *RV* I,32:[14]

> 1 I will declare the manly deeds of Indra, the
> first that he achieved, the Thunder-wielder.

---

[12]   See *Poetic Edda*, 'Hāvamāl', 138.

[13]   The notion of two cosmic phases is reflected in Plato's *Politicus* 269c-272b, where Socrates outlines the differences between the age of Chronos and that of Zeus.

[14]   All translations of the *Rig Veda* are from R.T.H. Griffith, *Hymns of the Rigveda*, 1889.

He slew the Dragon, then disclosed the
waters, and cleft the channels of the mountain
torrents.

2 He slew the Dragon lying on the mountain:
his heavenly bolt of thunder Tvaṣṭar[15]
fashioned.
Like lowing kine in rapid flow descending the
waters glided downward to the ocean.

3 Impetuous as a bull, he chose the Soma and
in three sacred beakers drank the juices.
Maghavan grasped the thunder for his
weapon, and smote to death this firstborn of
the dragons.

4 When, Indra, thou hadst slain the dragon's
firstborn, and overcome the charms of the
enchanters,
Then, giving life to Sun and Dawn and
Heaven, thou foundest not one foe to stand
against thee.

The battle with the dragon itself is described in detail
in the subsequent verses, but nowhere do we get an
impression of any dramatic action that may have
accompanied the priest's recitation:

5 Indra with his own great and deadly
thunder smote into pieces Vṛtra, worst of
Vṛtras.
As trunks of trees, what time the axe hath
felled them, low on the earth so lies the
prostrate Dragon.

---

[15]  Tvashtr is the artisan god who fashions Indra's thunderbolt, the
Vajra.

6 He, like a mad weak warrior, challenged
Indra, the great impetuous many-slaying Hero.
He, brooking not the clashing of the weapons,
crushed—Indra's foe—the shattered forts in
falling.

7 Footless and handless still he challenged
Indra, who smote him with his bolt between
the shoulders.
Emasculate yet claiming manly vigour, thus
Vṛtra lay with scattered limbs dissevered.

8 There as he lies like a bank-bursting river,
the waters taking courage flow above him.
The Dragon lies beneath the feet of torrents
which Vṛtra with his greatness had
encompassed.

9 Then humbled was the strength of Vṛtra's
mother:[16] Indra hath cast his deadly bolt
against her.
The mother was above, the son was under and
like a cow beside her calf lay Danu.

10 Rolled in the midst of never-ceasing
currents flowing without a rest for ever
onward.
The waters bear off Vṛtra's nameless body: the
foe of Indra sank to during darkness.

11 Guarded by Ahi stood the thralls of Dāsas,
the waters stayed like kine held by the robber.
But he, when he had smitten Vṛtra, opened
the cave wherein the floods had been
imprisoned.

---

[16]   Danu

12 A horse's tail wast thou when he, O Indra,
smote on thy bolt; thou, God without a
second,
Thou hast won back the kine,[17] hast won the
Soma; thou hast let loose to flow the Seven
Rivers.

The unusual birth of Indra – sideways from his mother – is described in *RV* IV, 18, this fact identifying him with Zeus, who also had to be hidden from his father by his mother Rhea in Crete:[18]

1 This is the ancient and accepted pathway by which all Gods have come into existence. Hereby could one be born though waxen mighty. Let him not, otherwise, destroy his Mother.

2 Not this way go I forth: hard is the passage. Forth from the side obliquely will I issue. Much that is yet undone must I accomplish; one must I combat and the other question.

3 He bent his eye upon the dying Mother: My word I now withdraw. That way I follow. In Tvaṣṭar's dwelling India drank the Soma, a hundredworth of juice pressed from the mortar.

4 What strange act shall he do, he whom
his Mother bore for a thousand months and
many autumns?

---

[17] The 'cows' refer to the solar energy of the universe represented as heavenly 'milk'.

[18] Cf. Hesiod, *Theogony*, 474-479.

> No peer hath he among those born already,
> nor among those who shall be born hereafter.
>
> 5 Deeming him a reproach, his mother hid
> him, Indra, endowed with all heroic valour.
> Then up he sprang himself, assumed his
> vesture, and filled, as soon as born, the earth
> and heaven.

We note in verses 2 and 3 above that Indra appears as a speaker in the chapter, but in verses 7-9 Indra's mother Aditi is the speaker:

> 7 Are they addressing him with words of
> welcome? Will the floods take on them the
> shame of Indra?
> With his great thunderbolt my Son hath
> slaughtered Vṛtra, and set these rivers free to
> wander.
>
> 8 I cast thee from me, mine,—thy youthful
> mother: thee, mine own offspring, Kusava
> hath swallowed.
> To him, mine infant, were the waters gracious.
> Indra, my Son, rose up in conquering vigour.
>
> 9 Thou art mine own, O Maghavan, whom
> Vyaṁsa struck to the ground and smote thy
> jaws in pieces.
> But, smitten through, the mastery thou
> wonnest, and with thy bolt the Dāsa's head
> thou crushedst.

However, we still have no indication of a sustained dramatic action that this chapter, or any others, may have originally represented.

Indra is helped in his fight against the dragon by the **Maruts**. The Maruts are sons of Rudra and Prishni (*RV* I, 85,2). Prishni is also described in the *Bhāgavata Purāna* (X,3) as the mother of Vishnu ('Prishnigarbha') reiterating the association of the Maruts with Indra/Vishnu.

The Maruts are described in *RV* I,37 as luminous, bearing arms, borne in a golden chariot driven by steeds, and having a 'spotted deer' as their mascot:

> 1 Sing forth, O Kanvas, to your band of
> Maruts unassailable,
> Sporting, resplendent on their car
>
> 2 They who, self-luminous, were born
> together, with the spotted deer,
> Spears, swords, and glittering ornaments.
>
> 3 One hears, as though 'twere close at hand,
> the cracking of the whips they hold
> They gather glory on their way.

*RV* I,64 gives a further glimpse of the gigantic size of these forces:

> 2 They spring to birth, the lofty Ones, the
> Bulls of Heaven, divine, the youths of Rudra,
> free from spot and stain;
> The purifiers, shining brightly even as suns,
> awful of form like giants, scattering rain-
> drops down.
>
> 3 Young Rudras, demon-slayers, never
> growing old, they have waxed, even as
> mountains, irresistible.
> They make all beings tremble with their

mighty strength, even the very strongest, both of earth and heaven.

4 With glittering ornaments they deck them forth for show; for beauty on their breasts they bind their chains of gold.
The lances on their shoulders pound to pieces; they were born together, of themselves, the Men of Heaven.

5 Loud roarers, giving strength, devourers of the foe, they make the winds, they make the lightnings with their powers.
The restless shakers drain the udders of the sky, and ever wandering round fill the earth full with milk.

The Maruts are described as 'giant' figures (*RV* I,86,1) that shake heaven and earth (*RV* I,39,10), thus the entire universe, and, breaking the resistance of 'mountains' and 'rivers', prepare the path of the sun. Thus, we have the following account of their action in *RV* VIII, 7:

4 The Maruts spread the mist abroad and make mountains rock and reel,
When with the winds they go their way

5 What time the rivers and the hills before your coming bowed them down,
So to sustain your mighty force.

6 We call on you for aid by night, on you for succour in the day,
On you while sacrifice proceeds.

7 These, verily, wondrous, red of hue, speed
on their courses with a roar
Over the ridges of the sky.

8 With might they drop the loosened rein so
that the Sun may run his course,
And spread themselves with beams of light.

The same chapter proceeds to describe the powerful
support given by the Maruts to Indra and Trita in the
fight against the dragon of material resistance, Vṛtra:

22 They brought together both the worlds, the
mighty waters, and the Sun,
And, joint by joint, the thunderbolt.

23 They sundered Vṛtra limb from limb and
split the gloomy mountain-clouds,
Performing a heroic deed.

24 They reinforced the power and strength of
Trita as he fought, and helped
Indra in battle with the foe.

There is also an indication in verse 31 that they
abandoned Indra at some point in the battle:

31 What now? where have ye still a friend
since ye left Indra all alone?
Who counteth on your friendship now?

though Agastya persists in imploring their attendance
at the sacrifice he prepares for them:

33 Hither for new felicity may I attract the
Impetuous Ones,
The Heroes with their wondrous strength

In *RV* VIII, 20, we perceive the association of the Maruts with Vishnu, who is the one who holds apart the heaven and earth formed of the body of the serpent Vrtra and traverses the entire universe constituted of earth, the mid-region of the stars, and heaven, with his three tremendous steps. The Maruts are described as 'Vishnu's band', suggesting that, at this stage, Indra is transformed into the solar force of Vishnu:[19]

> 3 For well we know the vigorous might of Rudra's Sons, the Maruts, who are passing strong, Swift Viṣṇu's band, who send the rain,
>
> 4 Islands are bursting forth and misery is stayed: the heaven and earth are joined in one. Decked with bright rings, ye spread the broad expanses out, when ye, self-luminous, stirred yourselves.
>
> 5 Even things immovable shake and reel, the mountains and the forest trees at your approach, And the earth trembles as ye come.
>
> 6 To lend free course, O Maruts, to your furious rush, heaven high and higher still gives way, Where they, the Heroes mighty with their arms, display their gleaming ornaments on their forms.

---

[19] The fact that Indra is the same as Vishnu is borne out by his epithet 'Vrtrahan', which is identical to that of the Iranian solar figure Verethraghna. The opposition of the Zoroastrian Iranians to Indra is thus clearly to the earlier violation of the Purusha/Chronos by Indra/Zeus. In Greece, as in India, however, it is clear that the same force that castrates the cosmic Man is the one that destroys the serpent Typhon/Vrtra. At the stage of the rise of the solar energy Zeus is called Dionysus and Indra Vishnu.

The sacrifice that Agastya had prepared for the Maruts and is the subject of the dispute in *RV* I,170 and I,171 that is discussed by Schroeder is described in *RV* I,86:

> 6 For, through the swift Gods' loving help, in many an autumn, Maruts,
> We have offered up our sacrifice.

> 7 Fortunate shall that mortal be, O Maruts most adorable,
> Whose offerings ye bear away.

In *RV* VIII,83, we hear the poet invites the Maruts to partake of the Soma sacrifice:

> 9 I call, to drink the Soma, those Maruts who spread all realms of earth
> And luminous regions of the sky.

> 10 You, even such, pure in your might, you, O ye Maruts, I invoke from heaven to drink this Soma juice.

> 11 The Maruts, those who have sustained and propped the heavens and earth apart,
> I call to drink this Soma juice.

> 12 That vigorous band of Maruts that abideth in the mountains,
> I Invoke to drink this Soma juice.

In his comparative mythological enterprise Schroeder associates the Maruts first with the Cretan **Curetes** and the Phrygian **Corybantes** who protected the infant

Zeus at his birth from his ravenous father Chronos by striking their shields and drowning out the baby's cries.[20] But there is no similar action detailed in the *Rig Veda* of the Maruts assisting the infant Indra. Besides, Schroder notes that the Maruts are 'brāhmanical' in nature, whereas both the Curetes and Corybantes are rather wild mountain-dwellers who are today called Kuratti (female of 'Kuravan') and Kuruvanji (clearly related to Curetes and Corybantes). It is possible that these tribal folk served in South India during the Sangam period (ca. 300 B.C.) as soldiers protecting kings.[21] But today both are names used to represent the gypsies, and the initial 'kur' of their names may even point to the Sumerian term 'kur', meaning 'mountain'. So we may assume that these entities are not Āryan in origin but, rather, Hamitic.

Schroeder points out that Athena too is represented in the Orphic mythology as the leader of the Curetes. Schroeder attempts to derive her name from that of the assistant of Indra, Trita Āptya, called in Avestan Thraetona Āthwyāna, and cites 'the remarkable consonance of the names that led significant scholars to relate Athene Tritogeneia, Tritonis Athena to Thraetona Āthwyāna and further to Trita Āptya.' The ambiguity of Athena's origins, however, seems to be supported by the fact that, according to Diodorus Siculus,[22] the name of Athens itself is derived not from Athena but from the (Hamitic) Egyptian city Asty, capital of Sais, whose chief deity was Neith, whom Plato accepted as identical

---

[20] See Hesiod, *Theogony*, 478-91.

[21] The term 'kuravan' is used for a 'leader' in Sangam literature such as the *Tolkāppiyam* and the *Silapathigāram*.

[22] Diodorus Siculus, *Bibliotheca Historica*, Bk.I, ch.28.

to Athena.[23] However, as the Egyptian priest in *Timaeus* explains, Athena was the original deity of Athens before the flood which destroyed the perfect Athenian state and Neith, who presided over the Egyptian Asty, was a derivative of Athena. Since Egypt survived the flood, and if Athens is indeed named after the Egyptian deity, we may assume that the Egyptians later colonized Athens with a religious culture that they had preserved in Egypt but which the Greeks had lost. This fusion of Egyptian with Greek culture may explain the inclusion of the Curetes and Corybantes in the story of the birth of Zeus and may be an indication that the earliest Phrygian and Cretan Greek mythologies may have included non-Āryan mythological elements that were later absorbed by the Āryans.

The Curetes are also possibly to be understood as a species of 'first men', who would represent the perfect Athenians of the antediluvian Athenian state described by the Egyptian priest in *Timaeus*. As Schroeder expresses it:

> These earth-born Curetes dwelt, one believes, in the Cretan mountains, a wise and kind race that supposedly first carried out the cultivation of sheep and bees, good herders and hunters, also inventors of ornaments for weapons, and the first Pyrrhic dancers or weapon dancers. They are also famed as seers.[24] In short, a respectable and meritorious race of primitive men who are considered to be the real autochthonous men.

---

[23]    Cf. Plato, *Timaeus*, 21e *et seq.*

[24]    *Ibid.*, p.541; Immisch, *cp.cit.*, pp.1601f,1604.

In any case, there is little to suggest that the Maruts are entirely identical to the Curetes or Corybantes, since the latter appear at the birth of Zeus whereas the Maruts accompany Indra mainly during his fight with the dragon in the underworld.

Schroeder relates the Maruts, Curetes and Corybantes also to **Mars** and the **Salian priests** of ancient Rome. The Salii were a college of twelve youthful patrician priests dedicated to Mars  who performed a dance called the *tripudium,* where the dancers move three steps forward and one step back. The three steps seem to point to Vishnu's characteristic three steps through the earth, mid-region of the stars and heaven of the newly created universe in order to free these worlds from the dragon Vrtra, who, in *TS* II,iv,12,2, is said to have grown and enveloped the three worlds.[25]

Plutarch[26] reports that the Salii beat their shields with swords. This is reminiscent of the dance of the Curetes and Corybantes at the birth of Zeus. Their association with Mars is similar to that of the Maruts with Indra.

It may be recalled that there were two colleges of Salian priests, one the Salii Palatini,[27] dedicated to Mars Gradivus, and the other the Salii Collini, dedicated to Quirinus.[28] This is because **Mars** himself

---

[25]   Vishnu combats the control of the three worlds by Vrtra with his three gigantic steps and thus allows Indra to hurl his thunderbolt against the monster (see A.K. Lahiri, *Vedic Vrtra,* Delhi: Motilal Banarsidass, 1984, p.195).

[26]   Plutarch, *Life of Numa*, 13.

[27]   The Salii Palatini had their seat in the Palatine Hill.

[28]   The Salii Collini were based in the Quirinal Hill.

is a development of Quirinus, who is the literal Roman counterpart of the Āryan Varuna/Xvarenah – the deity representing Ouranos sunk in the netherworld of Earth – since his name is patently similar to the Iranian Xvarenah. Thus Maurus Servius Honoratus, in his 'Commentary on the *Aeneid* of Vergil,' contrasts Mars with Quirinus: 'When he rampages, Mars is called *Gradivus*, but when he's at peace *Quirinus*.' This is rather like the verse in *RV* V,3,1 where Varuna is distinguished from Mitra: "Thou at thy birth art Varuna, O Agni; when thou art kindled thou becomest Mitra." So Mars Quirinus may be equated with Varuna and Mars Gradivus with Mitra. However, Mitra in the Vedas is not a god of war but of peace and justice. In *RV* VII, 82,5 and *RV* VI,68,3, Mitra is also contrasted with Indra, where Mitra has a quiet brāhmanical nature compared to the kshatriya Indra.

The original character of the Roman Mars may have been that of a deity guarding the peace of the Roman nation,[29] though he may have been adopted by the Roman military too as their guardian and thereby acquired warlike qualities borrowed in part from the Greek god of war, Ares. The warlike character possessed by the later Mars thus seems to be a merging of the earlier Vedic Mitra with Indra. It may be noted also that the Middle Persian version of Verethraghna (who corresponds to the Indic Indra or Vrtrahan, killer of Vrtra), Bahram, is associated with the planet Mars.[30]

Schroeder then points to the figure of Mamurius Veturius mentioned by the Salian priests in their song, the *carmen saliare*. This Mamurius is driven out with sticks on March 14, just before the Ides. Schroeder construes the significance of this figure as a representation of the old year that is driven out by the

---

[29]  See Isidore of Sevile, *Etymologiae*, 5,33,5 (see also Wouter Belier, *op.cit.*, p.88).

[30]  See R.C. Zaehner, *Zurvan: A Zoroastrian Dilemma*, Oxford: Clarendon Press, 1955, pp.147ff.

new. But Mamurius is the smith who forged the eleven *ancilia* resembling the one fallen from heaven during Numa Pompilius' reign that, according to legend, served as guarantor of Rome's sovereignty. Plutarch himself adds that 'Some, however, say that the song does not commemorate Veturius Mamurius, but "*veterem memoriam*," that is to say, *ancient remembrance.*[31] Further, according to Joannes Lydus, Mamurius was driven out not because he was old but

> the [original] Mamurius himself was beaten with rods and driven out of the city when, because of the removal of the original ancilia, difficulties had befallen the Romans.[32]

Thus the association of Mamurius with the shield and the dance of the Curetes and Corybantes is upheld and it is not clear that his driving out signified the passing of the old Mars, or the old year, as Schroeder, following Hermann Usener, proposed. Schroeder's preference for this interpretation is bound to his general understanding of these mythological figures as symbols of earthly seasonal changes.

Schroeder also considers the spirits involved in these events as souls of the dead that move through the air in wind and storm. This may have some relevance in the case of Wotan, who is, as we have seen, originally the same god as the Indo-Āryan Wāta/Vāyu, god of wind. Wotan/Odin is often represented in Norse mythology as the leader of the 'Wild Hunt' followed by the spirits of the dead. Later substitutions of female figures like Frau Holle or Perchta as leaders of this hunt may have been popular folkoric

---

[31] Similarly Varro, *De lingua latina*, 6,49.

[32] Joannes Lydus, *De mensibus*, IV, 49 (tr. M. Hooker).

transformations of the Valkyrie who accompany Odin to Valhalla.

As for Schroeder's association of all these spirits with fertility, this may have some support in the Dionysiac procession of maenads, sileni and satyrs who were transformed, in Roman religion, into the worshippers of the goddess of fertility Dea Dia and, in Germanic folklore, into the several vegetation spirits called Corn Folk. However, the association of the Salian priests with Mars may have originally been restricted to the dance of the Curetes/Corybantes around the infant Zeus – the god who will propel the solar force into our universe as the sun – and the fertility connotations that Schroeder invests them with may have been later popular accretions to the cosmic mythology.

Schroeder then proceeds to relate the Maruts to the **sword-dancers** of the Germanic lands and the Morris dancers of England. It is true that the Germanic dances are basically related to a narrative of the destruction of a dragon by a dragon-killer and of the celebration of this victory by a group of armed young dancers. It is, in fact, this phenomenon noted among the Germanic branch of the Indo-Europeans that prompted Schroeder to formulate his theory of the mimetic version of the *Rig Veda* which, according to him, preceded the later reduction of the verses to liturgical ones that merely accompany the soma sacrifices. Schroeder cites Friedrich Panzer's account of the progress of the dragon play in the Oberpfalz:

'In the border town Furth in the Oberpflaz,' narrates (Friedrich) Panzer, 'the 'stabbing of the dragon' is celebrated annually on the Sunday after Corpus Christi.' A king's daughter with a golden crown, her 'lady-in-waiting', a knight in armour on foot and a dragon made of wood moved from the inside by two men are the characters of the play. She sits on the 'hard stone' and narrates her distress to the knight, who consoles her and stabs, or kills, the monster as soon as it tries to catch her. Then she promises him, on behalf of her father, half of the kingdom. After twelve or fifteen hours, Bohemians and people from the Pfalz appear and take up in cloths the dragon blood that is spilt on the fields of flax, where it promotes growth and acts against witches. The Bohemians used to say that the dragon was the 'lindworm'[33] and the rescuer "Siegfried".[34]

The Germanic dances seemed to have been conducted mainly as a celebration of the new year in spring. The original significance of the defeat of Vrtra by Indra in order to free the solar energy from the constraints of the dragon of inertia seems to have been substituted in the Germanic lands with a celebration of the annual birth of the new year from the old.

The sword dances popular in Germany even today point back ultimately to Indra's fight with the dragon. In the sword dance on Papa Stour in the Shetland Isles,

---

[33]  A Germanic dragon that lives in the forests.

[34]  Siegfried (Old Norse Sigurd), who kills a dragon, is himself a mediaeval form of the ancient Germanic Thor, who battles the Midgard serpent called Jörmungandr.

for instance, the leader of the dance is St. George, the Christianised version of Thor/Siegfried. The sword dance may thus derive from Āryan origins and may be related to the battle of the Maruts along with Indra (represented as St. George) against the dragon.

The English **Morris dances** may be related to the Germanic ones originally, though their name itself probably dates back only to the time of Henry VIII and his wife Catherine of Aragon, since the Morisk or Moorish dance was popular in Aragon and Spain as a dance of victory over the Moors.[35] The celebration of Morris dances at Whitsun, that is at the end of spring and the beginning of summer, suggests that it is a celebration of the new year as well. This imitates the Germanic dances performed to symbolize the death of winter and the rise of spring. Schroeder further adduces the examples of the English figures of Tommy and Bessy as being cognate with that of Mamurius Veturius in ancient Rome since they too, as fertility spirits, are killed and then revived.

In general, we see from our survey of the evidence adduced for his thesis by Schroeder, and especially from the Vedic quotations presented above, that there is little likelihood of any dramatic representations that may have at any time accompanied the Vedic priestly recitations.[36] If there were mystery plays that preceded

---

[35] Schroeder, following Kuhn, associates the name of the Morris dancers with Mars, though this is uncertain since Mars is cognate with Old Latin *Māvors* and Oscan *Māmers*.

[36] The *Nātya Shāstra* also does not refer to any specific representations of the Vedic stories of Indra and Vrtra.

the Āryan fire-sacrifices, they cannot easily be deduced from the extant Vedic hymns. Also, it is likely that the dramatic representations of the birth of Zeus involving the Curetes and Corybantes in Crete and Anatolia were originally part of non-Āryan traditions. As for the dances depicting the battle of Siegfried/St. George against the dragon, these are clearly mimetic developments of the Vedic battle of Indra and Vrtra among the Germans and the Anglo-Saxons. But they do not seem, in their European forms, to have retained the cosmic significance of the birth of the sun that this Vedic battle (or the battle of Zeus against the monster Typhon) facilitated and, in a more 'down-to-earth' manner, celebrate the birth of the new year from the old.

# INDRA, THE MARUTS, AND AGASTYA

## RV I, 170, 171, 165

Among the dramatic hymns of the Rigveda – to which we now turn – are three which doubtless belong together and form in their totality a passionately inspired divine drama – the contest of Indra and the Maruts for a sacrifice prepared by the famed rishi Agastya and the finally happy reconciliation of the contesting gods mediated by Agastya. These three hymns belonging together have been somewhat presumptuously, almost fancifully called a trilogy.[37] According to our conception, they are not indeed three acts but at most three cohesive scenes and not even very comprehensive ones. Regarding their dramatic value, however, one can speak of three clearly articulated acts of an action and in this modest sense we can also finally agree to the designation of a 'trilogy'. In any case, it is a

---

[37] Cf. Johannes Hertel, *Wiener Zeitschrift für die Kunde des Morgenlandes*, vol.XVIII, p.153.

question of a very original and remarkable artwork of the Vedic time in three parts.

The understanding of the hymns has already been finely prepared by the researches of Oldenberg, Emil Sieg and Johannes Hertel,[38] but there remains still something to be done and we shall have to deviate in many respects from our predecessors. Oldenberg considers the hymns from the point of view of his Ākhyāna[39] theory and believes in supplemental and explanatory prose parts that have supposedly been lost.[40] For Sieg, the pupil of Geldner,[41] they are, in a similar sense, Itihāsa[42] hymns, but he adds the third and most important part (1,165), which was not yet moved into this context by Oldenberg, and has thereby rendered an essential service for the understanding of the whole. Only Hertel finally understood the three hymns doubtlessly correctly as a drama that required nothing for its explanation but the action.[43] We shall build further on this understanding.

According to the *Rig Veda* hymns, Indra is often enough accompanied in these battles against Vrtra and other evil demons by the Maruts, the belligerently

---

[38] Cf. Oldenberg's essay, 'Ākhyāna Hymnen im Rigveda', *Zeitschrift der deutschen morgenlandischen Gesellschaft*, vol.39, pp.60-65; Emil Sieg, *Die Sagenstoffe des Rigveda und die indische Itihāsatradition*, I, Stuttgart, 1902, pp.108-119; Johannes Hertel, 'Der Ursprung des indischen Dramas und Epos', *Wiener Zeitschrift für die Kunde des Morgenlandes*, vol.XVIII, pp.152-154.

[39] [Hermann Oldenberg (1854-1920), Indologist; Emil Sieg (1866-1951), Indologis and Tocharian scholar; Johannes Hertel (1972-1955), Indologist.] [N.B. All notes in brackets are by the translator.]

[40] Cf. Oldenberg, *op.cit.*, p.63.

[41] Karl Friedrich Geldner (1852-1929).

[42] [historical]

[43] Cf. Hertel, *op.cit.*, pp.138f, 152f.

armed youthful brigade of the storm gods. They sing his praises, they encourage him, they support him in battle. Indra accompanied by the Maruts – 'Indra marutvant' – is however not only well-known in the hymns, he also plays a decisive role in the religion. He is honoured with his escorts in the noonday celebration of the soma sacrifice with the presentation of a goblet and a recitation, both of which are named after the Maruts.[44] 'The Brāhmana texts – where they speak of this part of the sacrificial feast – trace the commonalty of these gods to the Vrtra battle in which the Maruts stood by the side of Indra as faithful warriors, like human vishas[45] by the side of their king.'[46] And they are doubtlessly fully right therein. This good accord, however, has not always remained undisturbed. One of the hymns of our trilogy tells us clearly what the cause of this ambiguity has been.[47] The Maruts once left Indra in the lurch in a battle! Very understandable that the passionately aggressive god flares up in wild rage against the faithless comrades and now does not even want to know anything more about the fact that

---

[44] 'Die Spende des marutvatīya graha und die Rezitation des marutvatīya çastra', see Oldenberg, *op.cit.*, p.60.

[45] [attendants]

[46] Cf. Oldenberg, *op.cit.*, p.60. I think that O. errs when he maintains on p.60 that in the *RV* hymns I, 170 and 171, the union of Indra and the Maruts should be traced back to another origin than that battle; and the reconciliation of the conflict described here perhaps is connected to the establishment of the Marutvātiya offering. No, the offering existed from the earliest times on the basis of the warrior comradeship, as the Brāhmanās state quite correctly. The Maruts make themselves unworthy of it only once through disloyalty. That determines the conflict. Only after Indra's wrath is fully displayed and the Maruts had fully conciliated him is the old relationship reestablished.

[47] *RV* I,165,6.

they should receive the sacrificial offering together with him – as is otherwise customary. That is the cause of the dramatic conflict in our trilogy, its prehistory.

The conflict itself is a fact, but already the oldest Indian tradition sways with regard to its motivation and even the modern exegetes do not entirely understand the situation as I have just represented it and as it seems to me to be natural and comprehensible. I must therefore say a few words about it.

Yāska's *Nirukta*[48] (1,5) – with which even the *Anukramanika*[49] agrees and which later authorities follow, represents the matter in such a way as if Agastya had originally prepared an offering for Indra but then decided to give it to the Maruts. Indra is supposed to have come by and complained in the first verse of the first hymn of our trilogy (*RV* I,170,1). [50]

That this interpretation simply cannot be reconciled to the text of the *Rig Veda* hymns was rightly recognized and established by Oldenberg, and Sieg rightly follows his opinion.[51] Yāska's interpretation also – apart from the text of the hymns – suffers from a deep inner implausibility. It is unthinkable that Agastya would have really wanted, on a whim, to present a sacrifice determined for Indra afterwards to the Maruts and would thereby have precisely provoked the wrath of the strongest and most passionate of all the gods – for the sake of the Maruts who were, in comparison to Indra, insignificant and secondary. In such a case the entire

---

[48]   [Nirukta is the linguistic science that deals with etymology. The treatise of Yāska (ca. 6th c. B.C.) on etymology is called *Nighantu*.]

[49]   [The *Anukramanika* are indices of Vedic hymns.]

[50]   One may compare the text of Yāska and the other authorities on this question in Sieg's excellent book, pp.110ff.

[51]   Cf. Oldenberg, *op.cit.*, pp.60ff; Sieg, *op.cit.*, p.110.

wrath of the god would have been directed against the foolish and disrespectful Agastya – of which however nothing is to be detected in the hymns. Further, Indra is really not the god who, in such a case, in such a blatant insult addressed to him, would come along to complain and whine.[52] A wild outburst of wrath, the flinging of the thunderbolt on the insulter, would be much more suited to his nature, indeed the only natural thing. Yāska's error consists in the fact that he ascribes a plaintively complaining verse (I,170,3) to Indra, in which Sieg follows him in a way that is hard to understand.[53] But this verse belongs, as Oldenberg already correctly recognized and maintained against the Indian tradition, rather more to the Maruts or it is spoken or sung by one of the Maruts, their leader and spokesman. For, Sieg has finely deduced from a verse of the third hymn (I,165,7) the fact that the entire troop of Maruts is not in accord with Indra but one of them speaks for all of them as a sort of choir leader or χορυφαῖος, and Hertel follows him therein with a decisive assent.[54]

---

[52] That precisely is the meaning of Yāska's expression: paridevayām cakre. If not for this statement one could be tempted to explain the preceding words sampraditsām cakāra other than as victory, with an emphasis on sam more in the sense of our interpretation: Agastya wished to sacrifice at the same time for the Maruts. However, I find in the *Petersburger Wörterbuch* no passage that could support that; sampra-dâ means simply 'deliver, surrender, give, provide', and Indra's complaint and whining agrees with that.

[53] Cf. Sieg, *opcit.*, p.113.

[54] Cf. Sieg, *op.cit.*, p.116; Hertel, *op.cit.*, pp.152,153. Indeed, before Sieg, Roth had already remarked in Geldner and Kaegi's *Siebenzig Lieder des Rigveda*, that 'Only some of the troop are imagined as speaking; in this way is explained also the vocative in verse 7 in that the speakers call upon the others to be witnesses to their words'. But he seems not to be quite certain for he adds in a rather feeble

The false interpretation of the situation in Yāska and the Indian scholars following him is however corrected now by still older texts, more important authorities in India itself. The Yajur Vedas and the Brāhmanās represent the process, in reference to the hymn *RV* I,165, rather in reverse so that Agastya wished originally to offer bulls to the Maruts but then slaughtered them for Indra or that Indra took these away and thus snatched their sacrificial offerings violently from the Maruts. Now the Maruts rush forth in rage, swinging the thunderbolt, but Indra and Agastya, or one of them, succeed in conciliating them once again.[55]

This interpretation which Oldenberg and Sieg endorse is, in any case, much more plausible than that of Yāska but it too does not agree so fully with the impression made on us by the *Rig Veda* hymns. There is nowhere mention of a wrathful, hostile rushing of the Maruts who, with the thunderbolt in their hand, wish to dispute their rightful claim against Indra or Agastya. And as little of an attempt by Indra to conciliate the raging Maruts. Rather, the Maruts are, according to what has preceded during the total action, rather

---

manner, 'However, even an accent mistake would be possible.' We have no reason to assume any such since it is decisively more probable that only one speaks or sings, not all together. We shall return to this later. Sieg, however did not generalize the remark but satisfies himself with the remark on the verse in question. But I consider it definitely likely that throughout only speaker speaks.

[55] Cf. *Maitreyi Brāhmana*, II,1,8, *Kāthaka Brāhmana*, X,11, *Taittirīya Brāhmana* II,7,11,1. In the *Maitreyi Samhita* and in the *Kāthaka* it is Agastya who slaughters the bulls destined for the Maruts later for Indra; the Maruts now charge against Agastya, but he conciliates and appeases them with the hymn *RV* I, 165. On the other hand, in the *Taittirīya Brāhmana*, it states that Indra took the bulls for himself; the raging Maruts are then conciliated by Agastya and Indra together with the mentioned hymn.

subdued and, far from wanting to stir themselves up, are immediately energetically repelled by Indra and appropriately made conscious of the fact that he – Indra – alone carries out the great deeds through his own strength and that the honour is due to him alone (*RV* I,165,7,8,10). Even in the third hymn, the last act of our trilogy, it is always Indra whom the Maruts wish to conciliate, not vice-versa. His mood is here already somewhat kinder than in the beginning, in the first hymn – not so wild, relentless, implacable. But it is even here at first quite hostile, arrogant and truculent. He makes the Maruts learn some truths, treats them politely, indeed almost contemptuously while they constantly strive to win him over and conciliate him. But he at least speaks to them again whereas, in the beginning, he considers them not worthy of being spoken to directly but speaks rather in general phrases or those directed to Agastya. The Maruts, who express everything very meekly, do not contradict him on any point, do not venture any harmful words against him, and agree humbly to the self-praise of Indra and are able to praise him in such a way that he is finally melted, his hard heart relents and is once again conciliated. Now he addresses once again friendly words to the old war-comrades and now, finally, even the bard praises even the Maruts with a light heart without having to fear that he would thereby draw upon himself the wrath of the frightful Indra.

However, even in one of the hymns, an attempt is made to conciliate the Maruts, but Indra does not do that but Agastya. The entire second hymn, the second act of our trilogy, is devoted to this attempt. Through Indra's wild and careless conduct Agastya is placed in a painful situation. With regard to the powerful god he cannot do anything but yield, do his will, otherwise he would without fail arouse his wrath. He must therefore give up a praise of the Maruts and restrict himself to requesting Indra that he reconcile himself once again with the Maruts. But thereby he has now insulted the Maruts too, who then express themselves immediately in that plaintively complaining verse that is erroneously placed in Indra's mouth by tradition and by Sieg. Agastya could not do anything else in the face of the wrath that Indra exhibits; however, the fact remains that he has insulted the divine troop of the Maruts and therefore he must try to conciliate them. That he does with the second hymn (I,171). He says to the Maruts that he has prepared sacrifices even for them but that he had to set them aside because he could not withstand the wrath of Indra. He praises the Maruts, requests them not to be angry with him, to grant him their favour once again; but he also praises Indra and requests him to abandon his wrath against the Maruts and to reconcile himself with them. But this attempt at reconciliation does not succeed. The third and last of the three hymns continues the reconciliation scene in which, at first, hard and contemptuous, arrogant and truculent words fall from Indra but, finally, the great god, faced with the humble mood of the Maruts, and the respect that they pay to him – as well as through the constant pleas of Agastya – is softened, allows his anger to fade and reconciles himself once again with his former friends and indeed even addresses to them some really friendly words.

Following this, I think that I must understand the situation in such a way that originally Agastya did not wish to sacrifice either to Indra alone or to the Maruts alone but to Indra and the Maruts together, to Indra accompanied by the Maruts, as was conventional, based clearly enough on the circumstance that the Maruts accompany Indra on his travels and in his heroic deeds, and stand by his side serving and helping him. But Indra does not wish to know anything of this, even if he does not yet say why: 'Neither today nor tomorrow will that happen.' He does not wish anymore to be celebrated along with the Maruts. He claims the entire sacrifice for himself, for he alone had indeed achieved the victory, without the help of the Maruts, who had disgracefully left him in the lurch. He turns against the Maruts in such a threatening manner in his ferocious anger that they already fear that he wishes to kill them and they try to placate him. They see that Agastya turns away from them and towards Indra and withdraw mortified – complaining that Agastya underestimates them and clearly does not wish to offer them sacrifices to them any longer. The latter explains to Indra clearly that he wishes to offer the sacrifice to him, praises and eulogises him, but requests him also to speak kindly to the Maruts.

But Indra is at first far from doing so. He accepts the sacrifice as being due to him in proud silence. But Agastya turns to the Maruts in the second hymn and tries, as was just described, to placate them and to explain to them that he indeed could not have acted otherwise. He requests both Indra and the Maruts to abandon their anger and to reconcile themselves to one another. After the reconciliation has been accomplished successfully in the third act of the trilogy, Agastya can, once again with a calm heart, following the traditional custom, sacrifice to Indra with the Maruts, to Indra 'marutvant'.[56] The bad accident that seemed to have

---

[56]    [accompanied by Maruts]

destroyed the traditional sacrifice and made it forever impossible has been smoothed out, has been fortunately removed, and has, further, the good consequence of having provided the material for one of the most vivid divine dramas, a passionately energetic mystery. The excitable, wildly flaring, stubbornly glowering Natural aspect of the proud, strong Indra rarely emerges so drastically as here. In this the Maruts do not play an enviable role but are, finally, graced with friendly words, and the wise Agastya proves his wisdom in the conflict that was hard even for him and for which he was not at all responsible.

1.

The first of the three hymns, the first act of our trilogy, *RV* I,170, is truly admirable on account of the energy of its expression, the compact coherence of its structure. The entire hymn consists of only five verses, but a small drama is played out in them. Only a single verse, the first of the hymn, is placed in the mouth of Indra but, with it, he masters the entire situation – naturally reinforced by the action, which seems very essential precisely here. Indra, filled with anger, rushes to the sacrificial altar where Agastya wishes to celebrate him and the Maruts, and shouts: 'That will not happen, neither today nor tomorrow!', that is, 'these sacrifices will not take place, I henceforth do not grant any share in them to the Maruts!' He speaks in general statements without thereby addressing either Agastya or the Maruts – with dark insinuations that must be understood immediately by the participants, the Maruts, and felt like whiplashes:

'You must comply with another plan and what you wanted can no longer be!' That is, 'the Maruts may only withdraw in disgrace! I cannot tolerate them!' Less clear is the second line: 'Who knows that which is hidden?' It seems that this wishes to express something like: 'Indeed, there are surprises! Suddenly things are revealed that one never imagined. You are surprised Agastya, you do not understand it – you do not know what is hidden behind. But I know what I want and what I do. That is enough. You will comply with my will without my saying why I will something!'

At the same time he turns threateningly to the Maruts, who have perhaps imitated his estrangement somewhat and not with an entirely good conscience. They act innocent as if they did not know why he is so angry. They point out that they belong to him like brothers, that he should be kind to them and not beat and kill them. However, Indra does not grant them a single word and even Agastya turns away from them or makes it clear through the removal of the offering destined for them that he intends to act according to Indra's words. Then, therefore, the complaining verse that the Maruts address to Agastya, even if he does not wish to have anything more to do with them and offer anything more to them. As the third party, Agastya speaks and at first avoids replying to the complaint of the Maruts and only assures Indra in clear terms that he wishes to offer the sacrifice to him, praises him and finally requests him, however, to speak kindly to the Maruts and then enjoy the sacrificial offering that is presented.

In the distribution of the verses among the individual persons I agree entirely with Graβmann,[57]

---

[57] op.cit., p.61.

with Oldenberg too almost, except that the latter leaves it doubtful for the second verse if it is to be placed in the mouth of Agastya or the Maruts. That does not seem doubtful to me since Indra's wrath is directed only against the Maruts and not against Agastya. Sieg erroneously attributes the verse to Agastya, but he seems to be more mistaken when he places verse 3 and 4 in Indra's mouth even though he is in keeping with the Indian tradition in the case of verse 3. Oldenberg has demonstrated the error of the latter. Ludwig's view, that the first verse of the hymn is to be attributed to the Maruts, is out of the question. It is indeed the glorious Indra verse which even tradition places always in Indra's mouth and which dominates the whole:

I present the hymn in my translation:

*Indra (appearing at the sacrifice):*

1. That will not happen either today or tomorrow,
   Who knows that which is hidden?
   One must comply with another's plan
   And our own plan is at an end.
   *(turns threateningly to the Maruts following him)*

*The Maruts (or their leader):*

2. What, Indra, do you wish to kill us?
   The Maruts are, however, brothers to you
   To them you must be kind
   And not kill us in battle.[58]

---

[58] The form of this verse seems to me also to attest to the fact that it is placed in the mouth not of a Marut chorus but in that of the leader of the same.

3. And you, Agastya?
   You, our friend, do you scorn us?
   We now know how you think
   You do not wish to offer to us anymore!
   (*they withdraw*)

   *Agastya:*

4. One must first prepare the altar,
   Let its fire be lit!
   Then we prepare the light of immortality
   And the sacrifice for you.[59]

5. Thou, Lord of wealth, bestow all your wealth,
   Grant generously to your friends, Lord of friends!
   O Indra, speak still as a friend to the Maruts!
   Then eat, as is fitting, the sacrificial offerings.

## 2.

After what has been said so far, the second hymn (*RV* I,171) does not require a long introduction. It is placed entirely in the mouth of Agastya and is directed mainly at the Maruts, and further also to Indra – apologizing, clarifying, appeasing, mediating, reconciling. That Agastya, along with this very worthy tendency of a priest to establish peace, shows also courage by repeatedly approaching the frightfully enraged Indra for reconciliation with the Maruts indeed deserves to be remarked.

---

[59] In the original the verb is in the dual. I think that Graßmann is right in his supposition that Agastya means himself and his wife. Further cf. Oldenberg, *op. cit.*, p.62, n1.

And now the hymn:

*Agastya*
*(addressing first the Maruts, then also Indra)*

1. I come to you and would like to pay my
   respects to you,
   You swift ones, I request your favour with this
   hymn.
   Enjoy yourselves, you Maruts, as you will,
   Put away wrath and unyoke your horses.

2. This prize song will favour you, you Maruts,
   I fabricated it for you in my heart, you gods!
   So do come and accept it gladly
   You are indeed the true promoters of faith.

3. Praised, may the Maruts be favourable to us,
   May Indra too be praised, the one rich in gifts
   You Maruts, rich in blessing, should
   All our days, like fine trees, rise erect.

4. There I must flee the violent one,
   I tremble full of fear before Indra, O Maruts!
   Powerful sacrifices were prepared for you too
   – We have removed them – excuse us.

5. The one through whom the Māna sons[60] gleam
   in the morning,
   Powerfully, when the dawn flames anew,

---

[60] Agastya himself is a Māna son. He calls himself and his kin
Māna sons.

You strong Bull, grant us fame with the
Maruts,

The powerful one, frightful alongside the
frightful.

6. You Indra, protect the warriors from one who
is stronger[61]

Be united with the Maruts! Abandon your
rage!

Be victorious with the gleaming ones, offering
to us,

We wish for power and habitation rich in
water.

3.

And now the third hymn, *RV* I,165 – the reconciliation.
The Maruts, following the kindly pleading invitation
of Agastya, approach once again in full splendour
the sacrifice from which they had earlier withdrawn.
Indra has at least not contradicted Agastya's attempt at
reconciliation and allowed himself to be glorified along
with the Maruts. That is already something. But he
still grumbles, is still scornful, he still does not address
a single word directly to the Maruts. He sees them
approaching and asks contemptuously why they come
in full dress, what do they want, who has invited them,
how can one make them stop their ride filled with hope.
He acts as if he had not heard Agastya's invitation at all.

[61] That is, from the enemy, who is physically superior to them but
whom they will be able to resist with the help of Indra.

The Maruts address him and ask him why he avoids them and does not speak to them, contrary to his customary behaviour. He does not at all respond to this, still arrogant, haughty and resentful; he just says quite generally that he comes to the sacrifice whenever and however he pleases. In spite of these little encouraging words the Maruts carry on the conversation eagerly and assure him that it corresponds to their wishes that he has appeared here and that they are also glad to be here. But then Indra's anger that has not yet been still breaks out once again and contemptuously he asks the Maruts where their desire was when they left him alone in the fight against the dragon. He alone is the strong one and the vanquisher of all enemies. They answer him – visibly embarrassed – not regarding the awkward question but praise his deeds willingly and recall that they too were many times with him as companions – and in future too may accomplish much united with him. But Indra turns them proudly back, does not heed this offer at all. He, with his Indra power, in his Indra wrath, accomplished all the powerful deeds himself. Not remarking the wound that lies therein, the Maruts agree with his self-praise and praise him as the invincible god with whom no other can be compared, who can do what he wishes. Self-conscious, defiant, Indra confirms that once again and praises his strength, but then he becomes softer – much indeed has happened to his pride. He tells the Maruts that their praise has pleased him, that he recognizes them as his friends and is pleased to see them. And now the sacrificer[62] can finally praise the Maruts calmly and

---

[62] The last three verses of the hymn have, in my opinion, to be recited by the sacrificer – or his appointed representative, singer or priest - for whom our trilogy with its relevant sacrifice is performed. Cf. also Max Müller, *Hymns to the Maruts*, pp.163,173.

present to them his sacrificial offerings.

Here now the hymn:

*Indra*[63]

*(staring at the approaching troop of Maruts)*

1. With what jewels do the Maruts shine there

   Who are of the same age and of the same family?

   What do they want? Where did they come from?

   Do they display courage desiring wealth?

2. Whose requests do the youths benefit from?

   Who has directed the Maruts to the sacrifice?

   They, who stride through the air like falcons,

   How do we bring them, arrogant, to a stop?

*The Maruts*

*(or their leader)*

---

[63]    There is no doubt that the tradition is right here when it places the first two verses of the hymn in the mouth of Indra as Sieg has already finely emphasized (*op.cit.*, p.115); Ludwig also follows him in his translation, and Lévi, *op.cit.*, p.305. Max Müller was definitely wrong in wishing to ascribe both verses to the sacrificer ('the actual sacrificer whoever he was', *Hymns to the Maruts*, pp.163,173); Roth in the *Siebenzig Lieder*, p.84. places it equally erroneously in the mouth of the singer. Graßmann seems to have viewed the matter similarly (see his *Rig Veda* translation, p.160).

3. Why, Indra, you great and powerful one,

Do you go alone, lord, what does that mean?

You converse with us normally when you meet us, the splendid ones,

What do you have against us? tell us clearly.

*Indra*

4. Prayers and songs I like, and drinks,

My courage aroused and already my thunderbolt is hurled[64]

They entreat me, their songs please me

The two horses take us to the sacrifice.[65]

*The leader of the Maruts*

5. Now then, we too, united with our comrades,

Autocratic all, adorning our bodies,

We, superb, prepare our spotted deer

Indra, you have appeared here in accordance with our wishes.[66]

*Indra*

---

[64] I interpret 'prābhrito me ādrih' in this manner; cf. also Max Müller in his *Hymns to the Maruts or the Stormgods*, p.165: 'my thunderbolt is hurled forth'; also *ibid.*, p.172.

[65] That is, 'Men come to me and I gladly follow their invitation to the sacrifice.'

[66] Sieg (*op.cit.*, p.115) translates differently, but not very convincingly.

6.  Where was this desire, O Maruts,

    When you left me alone in the battle against the dragon?

    I am the frightful one, the powerful one, the strong one,

    And I still defeat every enemy with my weapons.

    *The leader of the Maruts*

7.  You did much along with us your companions,

    With united force, O strong one,

    We shall continue to do much, Indra, you the strongest of all,

    With our strength, the Maruts, if we so desire.[57]

    *Indra*

8.  I struck down Vrtra with the strength of Indra,

    Through my own rage did I become so strong

    I liberated the gleaming waters for men

    With the thunderbolt in my arm.

    *The leader of the Maruts*

9.  Nothing is unconquerable to you, who are rich in gifts,

    There is no god alive who can be

---

[57] The leader of the Maruts first addresses Indra and then also the troop of his comrades.

compared to you
Nor will one such ever be born
Do what you wish to do, O mighty one!

*Indra*

10. Yes, let me alone have ruling power,
    What I boldly engage in I fulfil in wisdom
    It is I, O Maruts, who am the person who
    shows himself to be so frightful
    What I began Indra will already master.

11. Your song of praise has pleased me, O
    Maruts,
    The fame that you have prepared willingly
    for me -
    For strong Indra, who is used to contests,
    For the friend – as friends.

12. So, indeed, gleaming so brightly in front of
    me,
    Quite blameless, endowed with fame and
    strength,
    I see you thus, O Maruts, of a bright
    splendour,
    Yes, in this way did you please me, so do
    you please me even now!

*The Sacrificer*

13. Who is it, O Maruts, who now glorifies
    you?
    Friends, come to your friends,

You gleaming ones, inspiring the prayers,
Accept this sacrifice that I bring to you.

14. If the poet pays homage to you in order to honour you
If the wisdom of the son of Māna draws near,[68]
Come here, O Maruts, to the seer,
The singer wishes to sing hymns to you.

15. This song is for you, the song of praise, O Maruts,
Of the son of Māna, of the line of Mandāra,
Come here for refreshment, come to our sacrifice!
We wish for strength and a habitation rich in water.

We can and must think of this very lively religious drama or mystery, the strife and the reconciliation of Indra with the Maruts, as being performed in that most ancient Vedic age – which was not yet ruled by the later rigid ceremony that has been handed down to us and rather followed popular customs – with song and dance in certain sacrificial feasts. It was in any case a soma sacrifice which celebrated the victory of Indra over the evil cloudy dragon Vrtra-Ahi,[69] the liberation of the waters and the recovery of the light of the sun.

---

[68] I read 'ā cakre'; the son of Mānas is Agastya, who is the author of the three hymns.

[69] [Ahi is the Vedic counterpart of the Avestan dragon Azhi Dahāka.]

Dance would certainly have played a not insignificant role, especially towards the end, where everything ends in peace and joy. Indeed, Indra and the Maruts are, among all Vedic gods exhibited to us most clearly as dancers. After the conclusion of the reconciliation, the Maruts can perform in unblemished joy their dance, which must have been a weapon dance – because they themselves appear always and exclusively as splendidly adorned armed youths – which can also be equally called a dance of joy and victory, like most of such dances among the related peoples. A dance that is danced in honour of Indra, that celebrated his defeat and killing of the frightful dragon. Likewise, Indra himself also, the great victor, would have performed his dance of victory and joy as the wise men see him dancing to the Anushtubh metre at the end of another Vedic dialogue hymn, after the winning back of the sacrificial fire and the heavenly waters.[70]

Our three hymns are composed in the most conventional Anushtubh and Trishtubh metres, which we have presumed to be the most favoured dance metres, II and III fully in Trishtubh whereas in I Anushtubh predominates; only the last verse is in Trishtubh and the first, especially impressive, exhibits the Brihati metre, a modification of the Anushtubh metre, which, with its energetically thrusting third line, seems to me to be very appropriate.

Nothing certain can be said of how the performers, singers and dancers of our religious drama were, apart from weapons and jewels, otherwise adorned. We hear nothing in ancient India of masks and masked dances and therefore may hardly presume such accoutrements

---

[70]   Cf. *RV* X,124,9.

here. On the other hand, the *Mahābhāshya*[71] reports
that, during the epic reading of the Krishna legends, the
hostile parties of the followers of Krishna-Vishnu and
those of his opponent Kamsa appeared with painted
faces, some in red, others in black faces.[72] One may
therefore consider it perhaps possible, perhaps likely,
that also the performers of the Vedic dramas, here Indra
and the Maruts, were distinguished by such a painting
of their faces, especially since such a preparation even
in the mimetic dances of primitive peoples is nothing
rare.[73] However we have no further clues to be able to
maintain this with certainty.

It will be more important to survey similar
performance among the related peoples. The dragon
killer and defeater of the demons Indra and the armed
dancing troop of the Maruts, these are the major
characters of the present drama. Perhaps that leads us
farther.

The dance of armed youth, the dance with weapons,
especially the sword dance, is definitely attested in
different forms among the Germanic peoples from the
most ancient times up to the present. It took, and takes,
place on festive occasions and is, not seldom, combined
with a sort of primitive or folkish drama, or with
songs, speeches of the leader of the dancing troop, etc.
Sometimes even the actual sword dance is eliminated
and only a dramatic piece about 'sword fighters'
remained, as in Clausthal im Harz.[74] More often we

---

[71]   [The *Mahābhāshya* is a 2nd c. B.C. commentary on Sanskrit
grammar attributed to Patanjali.]

[72]   Cf. A. Weber, *Indische Studien*, XIII, p.489.

[73]   Cf. E. Grosse, *op.cit*, p.53f; H. Schurtz, *Altersklassen und
Männerbünde*, pp.100,101,105,106,218,341.

[74]   [Clausthal-Zellerfeld is a town in Lower Saxony.]

hear only of the dance. The performance is partly quite serious and worthy, partly also heavily spiced with humorous burlesque additions for the audience and the players. Christmas or Shrove Tuesday seems to be the preferred time for these plays. But also the May festivals offer many similar ones, and performances of this sort are repeatedly mentioned during weddings. A piper, a drummer, in other places perhaps also a fiddler, appear as musical accompaniment. The dancers are mostly clothed in white garments, perhaps also adorned with ribbons, laces, etc., more often decorated with bells similar to the Perchten jumpers[75] in South German districts.[76] Sometimes they wear hats or caps, sometimes these are found only among the leaders or principal dancers.

Already Tacitus describes the weapon dance of the Germanic youth,[77] who prance around naked in reckless play, jumping around swords and spears. He praises the art, the elegance of the performance. Later – as among the Curetes[78] – it is almost entirely a sword dance, which, in spite of many variations, is on the whole so strikingly similar in the different Germanic provinces and districts that the common origin cannot fail to be recognized and a performance based on a developed and ancient tradition cannot be doubted. Karl Müllenhoff[79] has provided the irrefutable proof of

---

[75] [The *Perchtenlaufen* is a pagan ritual battle celebrated in the Tyrol region of Austria.]

[76] Cf. Mannhardt, *Wald- und Feldkulte*, I, pp.540-548. Cf. also the bells among the dancing gods in Mexico in Preuß, *op.cit.*, pp;26,27.

[77] See Tacitus, *Germania*, ch.24.

[78] [See below p.70.]

[79] [Karl Müllenhoff (1818-1884) was a professor of German philology.]

this in a classic essay[80] and studied the sword dance in its different forms especially in Germany, Scandinavia and England up to the present. The following information is also taken in great part from his work.

In the cities of Germany, the performance of the sword dance was the privilege of certain guilds and halls, of the smiths and cutlers, who were related to this especially closely. But also schoolboys, cobblers or furriers or vignerons are mentioned. An interesting representation of the 'sword dance of the cutlers' in Nuremberg which was 'held on February 3, 1600, and previously in 1570' is found in Paul Geiger's *Schönbartbuch*.[81] 'The image shows a marketplace, with houses in the background, in the foreground two double circles of persons in white smocks or doublets who, tightly pressed on a mesh of their swords, bear aloft two quite colourfully dressed fighters. In the foreground, on the left, one sees a piper and a drummer and then seven sword dancers, six like the above in white jackets or doublets, only the first is clothed in red like one of the fighters, all with hats or caps.'[82]

The number of the dancers is moreover indicated variously according to the place. In Sweden, it is 6, just as in a description in Yorkshire, in Mokra[83] 9, in

---

[80]    Cf. Karl Müllenhoff, 'Über den Schwerttanz', (in *Festgaben für Gustav Homeyer*) Berlin, 1871. F.A. Meyer offers valuable additions to this, 'Ein deutsches Schwerttanzspiel aus Ungarn', along with 'Bemerkungen zum Schwerttanz', *Zeitschrift für Völkerpsychologie*, vol.XIX,pp.204-263.

[81]    [The Schönbart or Schempart Buch was a record, maintained from the sixteenth century onwards, of the Nuremberg Schempart festival. Paul Geiger (1887-1952) was a Swiss ethnologist who edited the journal *Schweizerisches Archiv für Volkskunde*.]

[82]    Cf. Müllenhoff, *op.cit.*, p.12.

[83]    [Mokra is a town in Upper Silesia in southern Poland.]

Salzburg 12 persons. In England, we hear sometimes of 15, in Hessen of 16-20, in Ulm of 24, in Überlingen of 32, in Breslau even of 36 sword dancers. But on the Shetland Islands, in Papa Stour, it is 7, same as in Nuremberg. And even the sword fighter play in Clausthal shows 7 persons.[84]

In the case of the seven sword dancers, one may indeed recall the fact that the number of the Maruts in the *Rig Veda* is given as three times seven.[85] Perhaps they are thought of as three dancer troops of seven youths each.

In Hessen, the sword dances took place, according to J.J. Winckelmann's description (from the year 1697), in Lent, but also during weddings, 'of which he has seen several with great pleasure'. The dancers – young provincials – wear white shirts, their hats are adorned with a ribbon of many colours and a white scarf, they have bells bound to their kneecaps, their arms are wound with a long hanging ribbon. They have a leader who speaks in verse to the gathering.[86]

Very vivid and interesting is the description of the sword dance of the people of Ditmarschen[87] that Anton Viethen[88] has supplied (1747). Here the old peasant tradition is cultivated especially in the ecclesiastical play in Büsum. The dancers wear white shirts, adorned and wound with colourful ribbons, have a bell hanging on each leg that chimes with every movement. The

---

[84] Cf. Müllenhoff, *op.cit.*, pp.19,25f, 30,33; F.A. Meyer, *op.cit.*, p.240.

[85] 'trishaptā', cf. *RV* I,133,6.

[86] Cf. Müllenhoff, *op.cit.*, pp.15f.

[87] [A district in Schleswig-Holstein.]

[88] [Anton Viethen was the author of the *Beschreibung und Geschichte des Landes Ditmarschen* (Description and History of the Province of Ditmarschen) Hamburg, 1733.]

principal dancer and the one in the middle wear a hat, the others dance bare-headed. The principal dancer, or king, holds a small speech at the beginning, the dancing or jumping begins with great skill and vivacity. In addition, drums are beaten.[89]

In the sword dance in Sweden that Olaus Magnus describes (1555), there are six dancers, clothed lightly with no coats or jackets and hats. They have a pipe and a drummer and appear mostly at Lent. Along with the *tibiae*[90] the description mentions also songs (*cantilenae*).[91] Nothing is said of the contents of the latter but one may surmise that they, like the songs of the hoop dance there, celebrated heroic deeds.[92]

But of special interest is the sword dance on Papa Stour (in Old Nordic: Pâpey in Stôra), one of the most remote Shetland Isles, which was extant even in the 19th century. A certain Mr. Henderson has copied a description of the same from an ancient manuscript about which Hibbert has made valuable observations in his *Description of the Shetland Islands*.[93] According to Hibbert, the sword dance on Papa Stour is performed mostly at Christmas, in the ancient Yuletide, still the principal festival of the island's inhabitants. There are altogether 7 dancers, of whom one is the leader of the troop. That is the 'Master in the character of St. George', thus of the dragon killer of the Christian Church, which has clearly entered in the place of an older mythological dragon killer. In addition, there is a minstrel man who

---

[89]  *Ibid.*, pp.21,22.

[90]  [flutes]

[91]  *Ibid.*, pp.13,14.

[92]  *Ibid.*, p.15: '*primum modesto cantu heroum gesta referente vel tibiis aut tympanis excitat, gyrando incedunt, etc.*'

[93]  Edinburgh, 1822, pp.555ff.

must strike up for the dance. The 'master' greets the audience with some verses and requests the minstrel man to play. 'The master bows and begins to dance, then resumes his speech during which the music stops; he praises his heroic deeds in England, Scotland, Ireland and France, Italy and Spain, draws his sword, dances and speaks once again and introduces his 6 champions and brothers dancing, whom he presents as Jacob from Spain, Dionysus from France, David from Wales, Patrick from Ireland, Antonio from Italy, and Andrew from Scotland and calls on them to perform solo dances as he had shown them before. All six are, (according to Hibbert), along with the master St. George, dressed in white shirts and armed with a sword.'[94] At the end of the dance that now follows, which is really artistic, the master approaches in a dignified manner and holds a small epilogue in verse.[95]

Here we have the most finely preserved sword dance in combination with a primitive folk drama which the dancers, the seven princely brothers and sword comrades, enact. But especially important and significant here is the circumstance that the dragon killer St. George emerges as the main personage, as the master or leader of the troop of dancing brothers. Of course, the killing of the dragon is not performed, but the hero praises his deeds and we may designate his dance too as a dance of celebration and victory. In any case, we have before us here the same connection of the mythological dragon killer with the weapon dance that we already know from the *Rig Veda*, where the dragon killer Indra appears with the Maruts related to him as brothers, armed and dancing. This same connection

---

[94]    Cf. Müllenhoff, *op.cit.*, pp.24,25.

[95]    *Ibid.*, pp.26,27.

that appears to us also in Greece – when Athena is supposed to have invented and danced for the first time the Pyrrhic dance, that is, the weapon dance, after the great victory over the giants –, an analogy that is even more striking when the Orphic hymns rightly make Athena the leader of the Curetes, the daimonic weapon dancers of Greek mythology. We shall return to this question later.

The 'sword fighter play' of Clausthal im Harz shows a strong relationship to the Shetland one since it also appears as a folk drama in which seven personages are presented, five kings, the servant Hans, and the original so-called Schnortison, who is killed only to be directly revived and dance again.[96] But here the artistic sword dance is forgotten and only its name has remained. Just as little do we find here the dragon killer St. George. Instead of him we have Schnortison, who is doubtless to be understood as a transformation of the ancient daimon of vegetation and fertility who must, according to the most ancient beliefs, be killed every year in order to be resurrected, rejuvenated, once again. We shall soon see that the connection of this figure with the weapon dancers is at least as old and as justified as that with the dragon killer.

But the dragon killer is attested more often on similar occasions. Indeed, the so-called Snapdragon,[97] whom others also call St. George, is one of the constant figures of the English Christmas and May festivals,

---

[96]   *Ibid.*, pp.33-35.

[97]   [Snapdragon was associated in English folklore with the dragon killed by St. George but also, in an English play of 1607 called *Lingua,* with Hercules: 'for when Hercules had killed the flaming dragon of Hesperia with the apples of that orchard, he made this fiery meat; in memory whereof he named it Snapdragon.']

and he is here not an incidental figure.[98] 'Mummers at Christmas perform a short dramatic piece of which St. George is the hero', it says in Hunter's *Hallamshire Glossary*.[99] On the so-called Plough Monday, according to Washington Irving's description, peasant boys appear clothed in original fashion, adorned with ribbons, who bear wooden swords – one of them clothed in coarse baize, his head wrapped in bearskin with a bell hanging and ringing behind – the clown or fool of the party. The leader of the troop recites an old ballad about St. George and the dragon: 'his companions accompanied the recitation with some rude attempt at acting', whereas the clown dressed in bearskin performs all possible antics.[100]

Even here we have, therefore, once again the sword fighters adorned with ribbons in connection with the dragon killer St. George and a primitive act, even if the sword dance is not mentioned and St. George does not appear personally but only a ballad about his dragon fight is recited. The boy dressed in skin accompanying the troop who plays the joker is an important character whom we shall meet often in different variations.

Sometimes St. George and a dragon appear vividly along with the so-called Morris dancers.[101] Even here we

---

[98]  Cf. A. Kuhn, *Zeitschrift für deutsches Altertum*, vol.V (1845), p.484.

[99]  See 'mummers'; cf. A. Kuhn, *op.cit.*, p.489.

[100]  In the *Mirror*, 26, p.42; cf. Kuhn, *op.cit.*, p.484. Plough Monday also falls within the Christmas season.

[101]  Cf. *Zeitschrift für deutsches Altertum*, vol.V, p.492. Kuhn has associated the name of the Maruts with that of the Morris dancers and also with the German Mahre, Mahrte and the Latin Mars, Martis, an association that has perhaps been much contested but is, in all probability, still correct, even if the derivation from the root 'mar', to die, remains very doubtful. That one thought of Mauren,

have before us the connection between dragon killer and weapon dance, for the Morris dancers, well-known for centuries and very traditional in England, who appear at Christmas and on May 1 until Whitsuntide, are weapon dancers or sword dancers. The Morris dance is a sword dance performed by young men with face masks or blackened faces which has been transferred in many ways to the chimney sweep guild – clearly because of their dark appearance. It is known that Adalbert Kuhn,[102] led by quite different thought processes, compared the Morris dancers to the Maruts already more than half a century ago. And it should at least be remarkable if we are led to the same connection from a quite different perspective. We do not wish yet, for the time being, to discuss in detail the difficult question since it will lead us too far away from the path to be followed at present. For us, at first, it is a question only of establishing the connection between the popular weapon dancers with the dragon killer, here St. George – a connection that clearly corresponds to that between Indra and the Maruts.

The dragon and dragon killer (Snapdragon and St. George), however, do not in general go necessarily with the Morris dancers and the sword dancers. The two appear often enough independently of each other. But their connection, or at least the connection of the dancers with the story of the killing of the dragon, is clearly not unpopular. Just as also the dragon killer

Mohren, Moriscos in connection with the name of the Morris dancers is very possible and was so much more apparent in that the Morris dancers were accustomed to blacken their faces. That was a very ancient primitive custom, much older than a later effort to represent Moors; cf. Mannhardt, *op.cit.*, p.546n.

[102]    [Franz Adalbert Kuhn (1812-1881) was a German folklorist and historian of the ancient Indo-European peoples.]

Indra and the Maruts in the Veda do not necessarily go together but are still commonly connected to each other. However, for the Maruts another connection is still more immediate and natural which was originally perhaps the closer and stronger one. I mean the connection with their father, the god Rudra, according to which they themselves are called the Rudras. This connection is indeed very noticeable in the *Rig Veda* though weak compared to the connection with Indra, the most celebrated of that age and those hymns, compared to whom Rudra, as we have already seen earlier, appears quite strikingly withdrawn. In the religion, however, the close relationship of the Maruts to their father Rudra, the great god of the soul and of fertility, emerges very clearly, especially in the autumn Chāturmāsya[103] or seasonal sacrifice – the feast called Sākamedha[104] – which is connected to a great funeral ceremony.[105]

Robin Hood, that very popular figure of the sagas of England, often appears as the leader of the Morris dancers, and indeed plays such a prominent role in the May traditions but also appears at Christmas, mostly along with his beloved, Maid Marion. It may perhaps be taken for granted after Mannhardt's researches, that we must recognize in Robin Hood a special form of the vegetative spirit who, like other vegetative spirits, enters in the spring and celebrates a marriage. The attempt to connect his name with that of Woden[106] was certainly

---

[103]  [The Chāturmāsya sacrifice is performed in four parts separated by intervals of four months.]

[104]  [Of the four sacrifices constituting the Chāturmāsya the third is the Sākamedha.]

[105]  Cf. Oldenberg, *Religion des Veda*, pp.441f.

[106]  [Woden was the principal god of the English from the time

an error. I would rather like to connect it with the appellative 'hood', that is, 'hat, cap' and understand its wearer as the hat-wearing leader of the warlike troop of dancers.[107] But even Wotan, who appears so often in the sagas as a wearer of a hat, is not by any means so far here as is now often believed[108] and, in fact, Kuhn will, even here, in spite of everything, be right, even if we do not wish to derive Robin Hood directly from the great god Wotan. Wotan is the great god of the Wind, souls and fertility who is associated with Rudra-Shiva and Dionysus-Hermes. He is, like the latter, doubtlessly developed out of a primitive spirit of vegetation or fertility who, like the other spirits of this sort moves in the wind and storm, expresses his life in the wind and, at the same time, stands in closest relationship with the departed souls that produce fertility, or originally was one of them.[109] He is therefore radically related to the entire troop of vegetation and fertility spirits and we cannot wonder if we see him often in sagas and traditions related to spirits of this sort or exchanging places with them. The folkish Woden was always much closer to the latter than was the great Odin raised to a god of the heavens of the Old Nordic mythology whose doubtless secondary image disturbs the comparison in many respects.

But we must return to the English sword dancers who can still offer us many interesting and important

---

of the Anglo-Saxon migrations of the fifth century A.D. until the conversion to Christianity in the eighth century.]

[107] Even the southern German 'Hutler' are perhaps to be compared here.

[108] Cf. Mannhardt, *op.cit.* p.546, note 3.

[109] Cf. my remarks in the *Wiener Zeitschrift für die Kunde des Morgenlandes*, vol.IX (1895), pp.233-252.

things. Thus Wallis[110] describes for us in his *History of Northumberland* (1769) the sword dance customary there that was performed at Christmas, 'the Yuletide of the Druids'. There young people go from house to house in strange clothes with music, perform the sword dance and receive for it small gifts. One of them is the leader of the troop. He appears in a 'more antic dress', that is, 'a fox's skin generally serving him for a covering and ornament to his head, the tail hanging down his back; this droll figure is their chief or leader; he does not mingle in the dance.'[111]

This leader, who at the same time plays the joker, is very noteworthy, already because of his costume, which recalls the earlier mentioned boys dressed in bearskin.[112] The foxskin which covers his head and back allows him to be recognized as a theriomorphic spirit, in all likelihood a vegetation or fertility spirit. One must think of the foxes often offered in the solar symbolic fire who are doubtlessly rightly understood as vegetation spirits in animal form. We meet a similar figure to these often, in England, under the name of Tommy in connection with the sword dancers, as a rule accompanied by a comical old woman, Bessy,[113]

---

[110] [John Wallis (1714-93) was an English cleric, naturalist and antiquarian.]

[111] Cf. Müllenhoff, *op.cit.*, p.29.

[112] [See above p.62]

[113] [According to an article in the *Newcastle Journal* of 7th January 1843, Tommy and Bessy wore 'the most frighteningly grotesque dresses imaginable; the former being usually clad in the skin of some wild animal, and the latter in petticoats and the costume of an old woman; it is the office of those two individuals, to go round amongst the company which collects to see them dance, and levy contributions in money; each of them being furnished for this purpose with a huge tin or iron box which they rattle in the faces of the bystanders, and perform other antics and grimaces to procure

in whom I would like to see a corresponding female form, the female fertility spirit become old who is analogous to our old Corn folk,[114] Rye Aunts,[115] etc. It can be deduced therefrom that it is often precisely this Bessy who is killed in the course of the play – just as it is the so-called Schnortison in Clausthal who is very characteristically resurrected, the Sterkader in the Lübeck play, and in other places the Fool, who corresponds to the English Tommy. That this killing was a very important and significant act – analogous to the expulsion of Mamurius Veturius in Rome[116] – has long been recognized and already Müllenhoff says, certainly rightly, that one may suppose 'that the performance in which the killing of the foolish boy or the old woman was lacking only bypassed it and was a shortening.'[117] It is the well-known killing of the vegetation or fertility spirit grown old that appears in very different forms, and has been transformed even to the killing or expulsion of the old year, the winter or death. The Scandinavian Yule ram, which is shot and, according to the verse of an original song, springs up once again alive and well and jumps around,[118] the wild man who is shot in Germany, in Thüringen, at Whitsuntide, and is allowed to be awakened to life again by a boy dressed as a doctor,[119] are well-known examples of the killing and reawakening of the vegetation spirit. That the death

---

subscriptions.']

[114]  [*Korndämonen*, corn spirits.]

[115]  [The *Roggenmuhme*, or Rye Aunt, is a female corn spirit with fiery fingers.]

[116]  Cf. Müllenhoff, *op.cit.*, pp.30,36; F.A. Meyer, *op.cit.*, p.229.

[117]  *Ibid.*, p.36.

[118]  Cf. Mannhardt, *Wald- und Feldkulte*, II, pp.196,197.

[119]  Cf. Mannhardt, *op.cit.*, I, pp.335,357,358.

and resurrection of Dionysus belongs to the same series of representations is perhaps not doubted by anybody any longer. But even in India there is something similar, and that – very characteristically – in connection with Rudra-Shiva. According to William Ward's description, there is a ceremony during the Shiva festival where a man must be killed who then comes alive again and dances while people cry 'Shiva, Shiva!'.[120] More common are the cases where we hear only of the killing of the vegetation spirit and not also of a reawakening at the same time.[121] But the representation of the rejuvenation or revival of the spirit is implicitly connected to the custom.

In the case of Bessy, we hear only of a killing, just as Mamurius Veturius, the god of the Year become old, is only expelled. The youthful Mars appears in his place. If Tommy and Bessy represent in manly and womanly form the old fertility spirit that has been discarded, we have to recognise, alongside these, the new, young, fertile, similarly manly and womanly, spirit – as already suggested – in Robin Hood and his Maid Marion, in the May Count and Countess,[122] etc.

John Brand (1777) describes for us how Tommy appears in North England (Northumberland) in connection with the sword dancers, as the Fool 'almost covered with skins, a hairy cap on and the tail of some animal hanging from his back.' He appears in a similar way in a later report from the mining districts, where the toilet of Bessy is described in a not less grotesque

---

[120]   Cf. William Ward, *A view of the history, literature and mythology of the Hindoos* (3 volumes, London, 1822), vol.III, p.22.

[121]   Cf. Mannhardt, *op.cit.*, I, pp.321,336,337,353,354, 357,359f.

[122]   [Maigraf and Maigräfin were Germanic counterparts of the English May King and May Queen.]

way. The importance of Tommy emerges here in the fact that it is his role is 'to introduce the sword dancers before the beginning of the performance with a sort of prologue song in Knittel verse.[123'124] He is therefore also, according to this representation, a sort of leader of the troop of sword dancers.

We must finally mention a very remarkable variant – of the so-called Giants dance in Yorkshire of which J. Kemble[125] passed on an unfortunately not very thorough report to Jacob Grimm. People in costume perform it in the autumn. It seems to have been a sort of sword dance since the main action consisted in two swords being hung and struck around the neck of a boy without hurting him. But especially important is the circumstance that the biggest giant is called Woden and his wife Frigg.[125] That doubtless shows us the mythological significance of the dance clearly. And if we see Woden himself appear here as a giant dancer, as the leader of a troop of giant dancers, we obtain a new and important trait in the image of the god that makes him more similar to the wild dancer Rudra-Shiva – a trait of which we hear nothing in the case of Wotan-Odin and which is, however, undoubtedly ancient and genuine. Only here too we must not think of the great god of the heavens of the Edda but of the more primitive but already very powerful spirit of the wind, souls and fertility out of whom the great god evolved.

[123]    [Knittel verse is a mediaeval German verse metre.]

[124]    Cf. Müllenhoff, op.cit., pp.30, 31; Das Ausland, 1857, no.4.

[125]    [John Mitchell Kemble (1807-1857) was an English philologist who specialized in Anglo-Saxon history. He studied under Jacob Grimm in Göttingen in 1731.]

[126]    Cf. J. Grimm, Deutsche Mythologie, 4th ed., p.252 ; Müllenhoff, op.cit., p.36.

And perhaps we may interpret the boy around whose neck the swords are hung without hurting him as the new-born young spirit of fertility that the swords support apotropaically, whose growth and flourishing the sword dance was, in all probability, destined to promote. Similar to the Curetes who hold their sword dance around the young Zeus, and the Corybantes around the child Dionysus, in order to protect him, as it has always been rightly maintained, and to promote it in its growth, as I would like to add.

If we see the god Woden with his wife at the head of the sword dancers or giant dancers and, in other places, the theriomorphic, fool-like Tommy who leads the sword dancers, then the latter stands alongside the former like the Fenris wolf alongside Loki, as a primitively related figure, a theriomorphic forerunner of the god of fertility. And if we see Shiva dancing with the skin on his shoulders, if the Thracian Dionysus wears as his headdress the skin drawn from the head of a deer or is depicted with bull's feet and a long tail,[127] such an appearance of the gods originally related to Woden recalls in some respects indeed the primitive spirit that is the forerunner of all three, and is never suppressed in the highly developed divine form.

Even Müllenhoff has clearly recognized and definitely stated that 'the significant relationship to mythology' was not lacking in the Germanic festival sword dance performances and as little were 'fables and dramatic content in the representations'. 'They seemed to have expressed the joy of festivity and victory not less than in Greece and Italy'.[128] He meant that 'the dancers in

---

[127] Cf. Rapp, *Beziehungen des Dionysoscultus zu Thrakien und Kleinasien*, pp.18,19.

[128] *Op.cit.*, pp.7,8.

the sword dance could have been earlier represented as famous heroes of the sagas or even of mythology'[129] and saw in the Yorkshire giant dance, even if the latter were really a sword dance, the most complete evidence 'of the connection even of the German or Germanic sword dance with the ancient religion and the ancient festive celebrations. And – he continues – this connection is not doubtful when the performance was held from ancient times around the time of the winter solstice and Shrove Tuesday only presented the beginning of spring. Then even the killing of the Fool or of the old woman doubtless has the same mythological-symbolic significance as otherwise and points only to the passing of the old year or of winter, just as the jubilant raising of the king in the play announces the victory of the new year. In short, this ancient Germanic performance shows itself to be essentially similar, indeed identical, to the Roman spring festival of the Salii[130] and the old servant Mamurius clothed in skins.[131]

The comparison is in the main doubtlessly correct and these sentences can, with some modifications, be maintained even today. We speak now not of the abstract conceptions of the old year or of winter but of the concretely conceived vegetation and fertility spirit that has grown old in the course of the year that, according to the widespread primitive view, must die every year and be renewed or be replaced by one that is new.

---

[129]  *Ibid.*, p.35.

[130]  [See below pp.98ff.]

[131]  Cf. Müllenhoff, *op.cit.*, p.36. Cf., in this context, also F.A. Meyer, *op.cit.*, p.261, who stresses that, alongside the doubtless commonly present mythological significance of the dance, that is, for the spring festival, the same could also have been originally of a profane nature. Tacitus' description supports this view.

But we must try to clarify a little more the mythological background of the weapon dance and the play connected to it. If we are right – as I do not doubt – in comparing to the Germanic weapon dancers – who sometimes appear united with the dragon killer St. George, sometimes, and more often, with an ancient vegetation spirit, or even with a god of fertility – the troop of weapon dancers of the Maruts that appears in the *Rig Veda* closely connected to the dragon killer Indra but originally belongs more closely perhaps to the god of souls and fertility who has been pushed aside in the *Rig Veda*, we must seek to obtain light for the corresponding figures of the related peoples – not only the Germanic sword dancers but also the Roman Salii, the Greek Curetes and the Phrygian Corybantes (whom already the ancients compared to one another) – which all taken together allow us to conclude perhaps a play of weapon dancers of the earliest Āryan times.

How the Maruts appear in the *Rig Veda* is well-known. More than 30 hymns are especially devoted to them, and even otherwise they are mentioned often enough and the image that we obtain of them here is an entirely uniform and clear one. They are storm gods who, armed with lightnings, race through the air and allow the rain clouds producing fertility to stream down to the earth. The mountains tremble and the woods bend when the armed procession of the Maruts rushes above them – the armed and warlike troop of youths adorned with shining jewels that we have already encountered. As winds, they are also singers and pipers and fare merrily forth with the well-known music of the wind. People have thought to see in the Vedic descriptions of the procession of the Maruts, perhaps rightly, the powerful natural phenomenon of the monsoons.[132] And in this way their connection with the storm god Indra seems very natural and almost self-evident. But, however clear all this may be, however finely and spiritedly the poetic conception of Nature and description of Nature of the Vedic poets reveal themselves precisely in the Marut hymns, one would still err if one wished to believe that the nature of the Maruts is exhausted totally in the natural phenomenon of the storm.

The close relationship of the Maruts to their father Rudra, the later great god Shiva, the god of souls and fertility, the god of death and of ghosts, points us from Nature to quite different regions, to the realm of departed souls. The armed troops of Rudra, of whom mention is often made in the later Vedic texts, and a great female following that is described with strange, dark, uncanny features, seem to belong to this world. But perhaps the same is true even of the Maruts, even they were originally perhaps none other than the troop of souls moving in the winds and storms, the ancient hunt or the raging army in ancient Indian form. Thereby we have arrived at an inspired supposition of Adalbert Kuhn that, in spite of many objections raised against it regarding its significance and justification, has not forfeited anything and, on the contrary, proves, on deeper examination, to be increasingly tenable and productive.

Kuhn wished to derive the name of the Maruts from the root 'mar', to die, and relate them to the Germanic Maren or Mahrten, the appellation of certain spirits or ghosts that play a not insignificant role in popular belief and are related to the incubus, but also to the sphere

---

[132]    Cf. Zimmer, *Altindisches Leben*, p.44; also Oldenberg, *Religion des Veda*, p.216.

of storms[133] and are, doubtless, originally the souls of dead men. He now understood the Maruts too as such, as one of the different forms of the army of souls racing through winds and storms, of the Wild Hunt,[134] of the Raging Army.[135] In their specifically warlike character, as armed and also really fighting men, they corresponded to the Old Nordic Einherjar[136] marching in Woden-Odin's convoy and they had to be further connected to the German armies of dead warriors, the *animae militum interfectorum*,[137] of which the sagas narrate on occasion that they slumber in the mountains and at certain times speed over the country in a storm wind.[138]

It is true that etymology does not provide any sufficient support. It is very possible that another root – 'mar', which means the shining, gleaming[139] – lies behind the words in question, as also the names of the Morris dancers and the Roman god Mars, that were presented by Kuhn. It is similarly to be admitted that,

---

[133] This last relationship through which the Germanic Maren come into contact with the sphere of the Indian Maruts is perceived through the fact that the lightning is their missile, for belemnite is called Maresten in Swedish and in German Marezitze. The so-called thunder broom is called Marentakken, Marenquasten, Marennest; cf. E.H. Meyer, *Germanische Mythologie*, pp.119,121.

[134] [The Wild Hunt is a motif in Germanic mythology wherein the spirits of the dead ride in a wild hunt led by Odin or, sometimes, by the female spirits Frau Holle or Perchta.]

[135] [The Raging Army is another name for the Wild Hunt.]

[136] [The Einherjar are, in Norse mythology, the warriors who have died in battle and are brought to Valhalla by the Valkyries.]

[137] [souls of slain soldiers]

[138] Cf. A. Kuhn, *Zeitschrift für deutsches Altertum*, vol.V, pp.488ff.

[139] The departed souls exhibit many fiery manifestations. Such are attested even in the case of the Mahrten; cf. Kuhn, *Norddeutsche Sagen*, p.142, the so-called Märtentrekken.

in the Rig Veda, nothing related to spirits or ghosts can be detected. Still, Kuhn's inspired intuition is in all probability right. The close relationship of the Maruts to Rudra speaks strongly for it and, still more, a series of cultural facts. And the image of the Maruts that the *Rig Veda* sketches does not constitute a total evidence against it. It is indeed very possible, even probable, that the poets of the Rig Vedic hymns naturalized the phenomenon of the Maruts to a certain extent and deliberately deprived them of their traditional character as spirits. We already know their aversion to the superstitious aspect of the belief in spirits. If they let a god like Rudra, who bore in himself too many and too deep connections of this sort, move to the background compared to the gods of the light, they could, on the other hand, have deliberately ignored and allowed to disappear the aspects of spirits inherited from the primordial Aryan age in order to direct their entire creative power to the poetic description of that great natural phenomenon that was offered to them by the powerful periodic storms of their new homeland, the monsoons. That would be completely in accord both with their vital feeling for Nature and with the idealizing tendency mentioned earlier of these poets, who sought to avoid the ghastly and the uncanny as well as the crude and vulgar – leaving both of these to the lower circles of the population.

Alfred Hillebrandt. who was earlier sceptical with regard to the view of Kuhn, was later convinced of the fact that there was still much that argued for it, and takes care to establish the same on better foundations.[140]

---

[140]   Cf. Alfred Hillebrandt, *Vedische Mythologie*, vol. III, pp.317ff. Hillebrandt's concurrence is of importance since he is both a thorough and a careful researcher.

In this he proceeds from the statements of the 5th book of the *Rig Veda*, in which the Maruts clearly appear as a troop of pious men, who, like other wise men of earlier times, worship Indra and act like other *manes*[141] who have risen to the status of demi-gods, for example, the Angirasas.[142] But he especially emphasizes, correctly, the special manner in which the Maruts are worshipped in the religion. The ritual books show clearly that the position of the Maruts in certain sacrifices is similar to that of the *manes*, Rudra or the spirits. Related to this is perhaps the instruction, for example, that one should present them outside with averted face.[143] Here the fear is clearly expressed that one feels before beings of this sort and that also emerges often in other circumstances, as in the worship of Rudra.[144]

The veneration of the Maruts takes place especially during the Chaturmāsya or four-month festival, those three festivals accompanying the course of the year which characterize or introduce the major divisions of the year and correspond to the natural three-fold division of the Indian year into the hot, the wet and the cool seasons. In each of these festivals, the Maruts stand in the forefront of the worship and there is evidenced in them, as Oldenberg has already observed, 'a series of ancient rites that have preserved the untarnished complexion of a folkish religion'.[145] Especially noteworthy is the autumn Chaturmāsya,

---

[141]   Chthonic spirits associated with' the souls of the deceased.

[142]   [The Angirasas are rishis who are considered to have composed several of the Rig Vedic hymns. The term also refers to a group of divine spirits.]

[143]   'vimukhenāranye nūcyam'; cf. Hillebrandt, *op.cit.*, p.319.

[144]   Cf. Oldenberg, *Religion des Veda*, pp.218,487.

[145]   *Ibid.*, p.441.

during which a great funeral feast, a sort of All Souls' feast, takes place and a remarkable sacrifice is offered to Rudra Tryambaka,[146] at a crossroads, the favourite place of departed spirits and ghosts. In general, however, this worship of the Maruts during the major changes of seasons is – as I must add – very remarkable and agrees completely with our view of their original nature as an army of souls that races through the air in winds and storms. For, even according to the belief of our people, the raging army bringing fertility, the wild hunt, passes through the air not only – even if especially then – in the twelfth month, at Yuletide, but generally in the major changes of seasons that constitute termini, the so-called Ember Days.[147]

The Āryan peoples know different forms of the army of souls that, according to their belief, march through the air in a frightening way but also as a blessing, because they produce fertility under the leadership of a male god of wind, souls and fertility or also of a related female deity at certain times in the night, rage in the mountains, or make themselves known in other ways. They are mainly the following:

1. The image of a hunting party, the wild hunt, the wild hunter, that is very commonly evidenced especially among the Germanic peoples, but also among the Greeks, in Dionysus Zagreus, and the passion for hunting of Artemis-Hecate, and that seems to have likewise not been alien to the Indians,[148]

---

[146] [Tryambaka is 'the one with three eyes'.]

[147] Cf. Grimm, *op.cit.*, vol.II,pp.766,776,782; Simrock, *Deutsche Mythologie*, pp.240,242,246. (Ember Days are quarterly periods of fasting in the Catholic Church as well as in the Anglican Church.

[148] Cf. Winternitz in *Wiener Zeitschrift für die Kunde des Morgenlandes*, vol.XIV, pp.243-264.

2. the image of a male army armed in a warlike manner, of the *animae militum interfectorum*, that concerns us here specifically and that perhaps corresponds to a female warlike army in the Amazons of Artemis,

3. the image of an ecstatically inspired, shouting and raging troop of women, that emerge bound with snakes, or even hiss like snakes, tear apart live animals and swallow their meat, etc. The procession of the Maenads and Hyades in Greece, the female army troops – the Senās – of Rudra in India, are the classical examples of this,

4. the image of a procession of theriomorphic, mostly phallic spirits of fertility, who are accompanied by beautiful women as a supplement, the Thiasos of Dionysus with his satyrs, silens and nymphs, the troops of the Gandharvas and Apsaras belong here,

5. the image of a troop of children's souls, which is familiar to the German sagas, which I have however encountered even among the Latvian people.

Sometimes some of these images overlap one another and are confused but, on the whole, they can be quite clearly held separately.

The procession of the Maruts appears as a thoroughly characteristic representative of the second group, which we already know among the Germanic peoples, but will meet also among other Āryan peoples. Naturally, I cannot go into the details of comparative mythological research here but only give a presentation in broad strokes that hopefully will nevertheless be capable of serving conviction.[149]

In Greece, to the young troop of weapon dancers of the Maruts clearly correspond the Curetes, those dancing spirits of Cretan tradition who, once again, resemble the Phrygian Corybantes so strikingly that already the Greeks equated them to each another.

The Curetes are demi-divine spirits living in the mountains who belong to the immediate entourage of the mother of the gods and the mountain goddess Rhea, just as the Phrygian Corybantes are immediately attached to the Phrygian mother of the gods Cybele related to Rhea,.[150] One imagines them as a troop of armed youths – which is attested moreover by their name, which in Homer, as an appellative, designates the team of youths of the Greek army.[151] The characteristic of this troop that emerges most often or, more accurately, the activity that characterizes them most fully, is the dance, the weapon dance, the Pyrrhic or, as the Cretans call it, the Prylis. 'The dance of the Curetes', says Immisch, 'is the main component and core of the mythopoeia related to them to such an extent that everything else recedes compared to it.'[152] They are spirited dancers, as Hesiod already designates them in a fragment contained in Strabo, where he at the same time presents them as close relations of

---

[149]   I intend to publish more detailed arguments in a special work *Altarische Religion*, of which at present around $2^{1}/_{2}$ volumes have been mainly completed in manuscript.

[150]   Cf. Preller, *Griechische Mythologie*, 3rd ed., I, pp.106,541; Immisch in Roscher's Mythologisches Lexikon, 'Kureten', p.1594.

[151]   [See Homer, *Iliad*, XIX,193, where Agamemnon uses the term 'Curetes' in describing an elite band of Achaean warriors.]

[152]   Cf. Immisch, *op.cit.*, p.1613.

the mountain nymphs and satyrs.[153] One sees them represented on many monuments as dancing armed with swords and shields – dancing around the child Zeus, just as the Corybantes dance around the child Dionysus. Indeed the myth related that his mother Rhea had hidden the newborn Zeus from the pursuit of his father Cronos in a cave of the wooded mountains, but the Curetes dancing around the child, striking their shields with their swords, had through such a noise drowned out the crying of the child and in this way protected him from the danger threatening him. The mythological significance of the dance of the Curetes was, accordingly, interpreted by Preller and Immisch as an apotropaic one that wards off evil. That may be right, but this dance may perhaps have possessed, alongside such a negative, defensive and deterrent significance, also originally a positive one awakening and creating life and fertility as is often enough attested and well-known to us regarding dance in particular and kinetic magic in general.[154]

This idea is suggested to us by the circle of gods to which the Curetes as well as the Corybantes belong. The great Mother, the mother of the gods, Rhea-Cybele – a figure that, along with her entourage, clearly goes back to that prehistory where Greeks and Phrygians still belonged together ethnically – was a great goddess of life and of fertility in Nature – in human and animal life as well as in vegetable – a sort of female counterpart to the great god of fertility Dionysus, with whom she is often and closely enough related and connected. The

---

[153]   Cf. Preller, *op.cit.*, I, p.540n; Immisch, *op.cit.*, p.1595.

[154]   The association of the protecting, defending significance with the positively promoting one is attested in many customs, which I cannot discuss more closely here.

life-awakening power of this orgiasm however may be considered as being proved a long time ago. And if now the Curetes belong closely with this mother of the gods, if they may be considered, following the evidence of Hesiod, as close relatives of the mountain nymphs and satyrs, those well-known spirits of fertility, then the suggestion to interpret their nature as a similarly essentially related one is irresistible. Thus we will be inclined to understand the Curetes as well as the Corybantes belonging to Cybele and Dionysus as spirits fostering life and growth that not only protect the new-born god but, through their magical religious dance, allow him to grow and become strong. And it is entirely in keeping with this presupposition when the Orphic mysticism celebrates the Curetes as life-giving, life producing spirits promoting growth and fertility[155] and considers it as sharing in 'the production of all life'.[156]

But the Orphic mysticism offers us another important and noteworthy trait to the image of the Curetes that has up to now not been sufficiently valued or perhaps understood only as the mere 'speculation of rationalizing theology'[157] – a trait that appears in its proper light and gives evidence of its importance for them only through comparison. That mysticism understands the Curetes as wind spirits that promote or even destroy life and growth 'according to whether they fly raging and destroying or in a fructifying manner.'[158]

---

[155] As ζῳογόνος and τροφέες, ψυχοτρόφος, ὡροτρόφος, φερέκαρπος, cf. Immisch, cp.cit., pp.1622,1623.

[156] ὅλης ζῳῆς ζῳογονία, cf Immisch, op.cit., p.1623.

[157] Cf. Immisch, op.cit., p.1622.

[158] They are ζῳογόνοι πνοιαί, πνοιαὶ ἀένοι, are εὔπνοοι, are τροφέες τε καὶ αὐτ' ὀλετῆρες, cf. Immisch, op.cit., pp.1622,1623.

As wind gods, they are also protective gods of seafarers.[159] But if this is an old trait – as I do not doubt it is – then it is obvious that the relation of this troop of armed, dancing youths to the troop of the Maruts is enriched further with a remarkable trait and is more strongly established thereby, that even the association of these spirits to the larger group of fertility gods – who reveal thus in many ways the clearest relationship to the phenomenon of the wind – is expressed in a more definite way.

If the Curetes show, alongside the blessing imparting trait also one that is dangerous and threatening, this dual character is known to us also in the Maruts. In both the semi-divine troops, the Indian as well as the Greek, however the benevolent predominates over the bad and dangerous aspect. Indeed, the Maruts are actually healing gods, doctors, like their father Rudra and a corresponding characteristic is also not quite lacking in the Curetes and Corybantes. And if the Curetes, like Rhea-Cybele, dwell in the mountains, it may also be recalled that the *Rig Veda* says of the troop of Maruts that they have their location in the mountains[160] – a characteristic that emerges even more strongly in their father Rudra-Shiva as well as in his wife, Durgā-Pārvati. We know it also in Artemis and Dionysus – insofar as he moves in the mountains –, in Woden-Odin, Mother Holle[161] and the Germanic army of souls. The wind

---

[159]   Cf. Immisch, *op.cit.*, p.1623.

[160]   Cf. *RV* VIII,83,12 'mārutam ganām girishthām'. On the close relationship of the Maruts to the mountains, see also Pischel, *Zeitschrift der deutschen morgenländischen Gesellschaft*, vol.35, p.717.

[161]   [Frau Holle, or Mutter Holle, or Holda, is, in Germanic legend, a leader of nocturnal female spirits. Sometimes she is represented as the leader of the Wild Hunt, a position normally occupied by Odin. She was characterized as a witch by the Catholic Church.]

comes from the mountains – wind gods and souls dwell by preference in the mountains.

The armed, dancing troop of youths of the Curetes, with their iron shields,[162] reminds us immediately of the armed dancing group of the Romans, the Salii. That already struck the ancients too. Already Dionysus of Halicarnassus draws this comparison,[163] and we shall soon see that the same is completely appropriate even if it is, among the Romans, a matter of a noble group of priests and among the Greeks of mythological beings. Much more striking is it when a Roman who is to be taken so seriously as Nigidius Figulus[164] compares the Curetes to the Lares.[165] And yet, on closer inspection, there speaks in fact more than one element for the correctness of this interpretation, according to which we would have to recognize in the Curetes, in the final analysis, a particularly formed troop of the souls of ancestors.[166] If it is rightly grounded, the comparison with the Maruts is, in a surprising way, completely affirmed and the proof of the identity of the Curetes with the warlike armed Indian wind spirits finally decided. For I consider it as no longer doubtful that the

---

[162]  Χαλκάσπιδες; cf. Preller, *op.cit.*, I, p.541.

[163]  Dionysus Halicarnassus, 2,70; cf Immisch, *op.cit.*, pp.1606,1613.

[164]  [Publius Nigidius Figulus (ca.98-45 B .C.) was a praetor and military officer and a friend of Cicero. As a scholar he produced several works on diverse subjects such as linguistics, astronomy and astrology. He was a keen Pythagorean.]

[165]  Cf. Immisch, *op.cit.*, p.1613, also p.1614: Hesychius, λάρεις, λάραβες, τοὺς κυρίτας (=Curetes) ῥωμαῖος οὕτως.

[166]  The character of the Lares as departed souls that was clear yet to Varro has quite wrongly been doubted recently. The doubtless correct view of the ancients is now defended with good reason by Hugo Ehrlich in the valuable essay series, 'Zur Mythologie', *Zeitschrift für vergleichende Sprachforschung*, vol.41, sec. 3, pp.295-304.

latter are to be understood in their fundamental nature as a particular form of the army of souls.

Here the circumstance is particularly important that, alongside the predominantly apparent image of the Curetes as armed, dancing spirits, another image was present according to which they were considered the first men, a sort of primordial race, sprung from the earth like trees, and at the same time the first worshippers of Zeus – quite similar to the way the Corybantes too were at the same time considered the first creatures and the first worshippers and priests of the great Mother, who likewise – according to an ancient poem – supposedly sprang from the earth like trees.[167] These earth-born Curetes dwelt, one believes, in the Cretan mountains, a wise and kind race that supposedly first carried out the cultivation of sheep and bees, good herders and hunters, also inventors of ornaments for weapons and the first Pyrrhic dancers or weapon dancers. They are also famed as seers.[168] In short, a respectable and meritorious race of primitive men who are considered to be the real autochthonous men.

That these ideas do not have the least historic-ethnographic value may be taken for granted. On the other hand, one would doubtless go too far in the opposite direction if one cast these aside as just worthless and if one wished to ignore them as meaningless games of the fancy. But in them is expressed with great clarity the idea that the Curetes were originally men, men of prehistory – and this idea does not contradict in any aspect the standard image of these beings as dancing spirits, rather it agrees with the same in a thoroughly

---

[167] Cf. Preller, *op.cit.*, I, pp.529,540,106.

[168] *Ibid.*, p.541; Immisch, *op.cit.*, pp.1601f,1604.

natural manner. If we understand the Curetes, as well as the Corybantes closely related to them, as a special, and definitely expressed form of the army of souls, if we suppose that they were this at least originally and if this characteristic was later obscured – just as in the case of the Maruts – then everything is in order and there is no contradiction at all. Then we understand the close relationship of the Curetes and Corybantes to the Dionysiac circle better than before. Then their relationship to the Maruts[169] and the corresponding Germanic figures becomes clearer than hitherto and we obtain, for Greece, that idea of the army of souls that we still lacked: alongside (1) the idea of the wild hunt, (2) the idea of dancing and prancing spirits in the shape of rams and horses, (3) the idea of the orgiastic female army of the Maenads and Hyiades, the idea also of an armed, dancing and leaping troop of warriors.

If we may – as I think we may – consider even the Orphic characteristic of the Curetes as wind gods as being well grounded, then we would have before us in the Curetes clearly a special group of the important gods or spirits of wind, souls and fertility among which even the Maruts are to be counted. In the case of the Maruts, through a special development in the hymns of the *Rig Veda*, the wind nature has emerged strongly in the foreground, in the case of the Curetes and the Corybantes the magical-religious weapon dance. Basically, however, they are the same beings which the Āryan prehistory must have already known.

---

[169]    I recall once again the fact that the Maruts appear in the 5th book of the *Rig Veda* as worshippers of Indra who sing to him, sacrifice to him as a brāhmanical race that is bound to the worship of Indra (cf. Hillebrandt, *Vedische Mythologie*, vol.III, pp.310,318); similarly, the Curetes are characterized as the first worshippers and priests of Zeus, see Preller, *op.cit.*, I, pp.106,540.

But one more fact of a religious sort is important for us. It is certain that the dances of the Corybantes were performed by priestly representatives. There is not the least reason to confuse these human dancers with the daemonic and godly, the actual, Corybantes, or indeed to explain the latter only as mythological representatives of the former. Rather, we have merely to do with the interesting religious fact that the Corybantes with their dances were performed by priests in the mysteries as well as in the processions. And if the same is not directly proven in the case of the Curetes too, it is highly likely and one may, with Immisch, confidently suppose that even in their rituals 'there was not lacking a reproduction of the Cureten dance by weapon dancers'.[170] But it was essentially the same thing that we were led to also in the case of the Maruts – indeed, as regards their form, we saw the Marut troop emerging, acting and speaking, or singing, in a small religious drama that the *Rig Veda* has preserved for us, under the direction of a leader. There is no doubt that they were there acted by human or priestly persons that brought vividly to life the armed, dancing troop of youths of the Maruts. And one may perhaps suppose with certainty that – as in the case of the Corybantes and Curetes – the weapon dance was something essential, even if the ritual fixed in a later age does not know or report anything about this, as it does not in general of any cultic drama. We already know that in the *Rig Veda* the Maruts appear to their worshippers jumping and dancing spiritedly[171] and perhaps nothing is so obvious than the supposition that here there was before the poet the image of a mimetic-dramatic religious dance of

---

[170]  Cf. Immisch, *op.cit.*, pp.1611,1614,1610.

[171]  Cf. above pp.54ff; *RV* I,166,2.

armed youths or priests – just as the Corybantes were seen dancing physically in Phrygia and the Curetes in Crete.

But for the Curetes the Orphic hymns offer another interesting trait which deserves our attention. Even in these hymns the weapon dance forms – as elsewhere – the core of the myth of the Curetes, but noteworthy is also the closer relationship emergent here of Athena to these daemonic weapon dancers. Athena appears directly as their leader, as the inventor of the rhythmic choral dance to honour whom the Curetes crowned themselves with olives.[172] In order to correctly evaluate the significance of this connection it is not enough to point to Athena as the inventor of the weapon dance. We should rather wish to attempt to illuminate the character of this deity from the point of view of comparative mythology. This can be done here only in brief aspects but is necessary here.

We must fill it out a little further.

In the *Rig Veda*, in connection with Indra, there often appears a remarkable old god, whose persona – in many respects, obscure, fragmentary, contradictory, though clearly recognizable in its outlines – reaches back in its roots doubtless to a primordial prehistory and may have once played a bigger role. This is Trita, who also bears the epithet Āptya – that is, the one belonging to waters or originating from the waters – wherewith doubtless the waters of the clouds are meant since he – a god of lighting and thunder related to Indra and a friend of Indra – has a doubtlessly clear relationship to these. He often appears as a sort of precursor of Indra who, like the latter – and earlier than him – killed the evil cloud spirits and freed the streams

---

[172] Cf. Immisch, *op.cit.*, p.1622.

of water. One gets this impression when, for example, in the *Rig Veda* it says that Indra, the bearer of the thunderbolt, clove the defences of the Vala like Trita.[173] There Trita indeed appears clearly as the prototype of such heroic acts known already before Indra. But in others passages of the Vedic hymns we see Trita rather more acting on Indra's commission or strengthened by Indra's force as his helper and servant; or Indra favours Trita in his work and helps him to victory. Similarly changing, apparently contradictory, images appear when it is once said that the roaring Trita gifted the lightning to the Maruts,[174] but in an another passage rather that the Maruts fortify the strength and courage of the battling Trita. These are clearly related, comradely forces of the airy region, that alternately help and advance one another in the powerful battle of lightning and thunderstorm.

Trita appears related to Indra also in the fact that he stands in closest relationship to Soma. Just like Indra, Trita also owes the strength of his heroic act, the smashing of Vrtra, to the Soma drink.[175] Soma is attributed to Trita as well as to Indra.[176] Indeed, Trita himself appears as the one who prepares the Soma, and Indra drinks the heavenly intoxicant with Trita Āptya, as also, moreover, in the company of Vishnu and the Maruts.[177]

But Trita is also a wise, knowing god. Of him – who is in the passage in question identified even with Varuna – it is once said that all wisdom is in him, just

---

[173]   *RV* I,52,5.

[174]   *RV* V,54,2.

[175]   *RV* I,187,1.

[176]   *RV* IX,34,4.

[177]   *RV* VIII,12,16.

as the hub is set in the wheel.[178] The singer declaims 'the wise Trita Āptya!' in another passage.[179]

Once there appears in the *Rig Veda* also a clearly related god, Traetona, in an unfortunate fight with the demon Dāsa.[180] His name is clearly a patronymic for a first name Tritan, which may be considered a variant of Trita. He would therefore be a son of Trita or Tritan.

But such a son of Trita plays an important role also in the Avesta and, further, also in the Persian heroic sagas, and in general here it is most interesting and significant to compare the related myths and sagas of the Persian kinsfolk.

We find Thrita and Āthwya mentioned as two heroes of prehistory who are among the first preparers and worshippers of Haoma, that divinized holy intoxicant that is originally identical to the Indian Soma. Thrita is identical to the Indian Trita, Āthwya to Āptya[181] and there is here only the difference that the Vedic Trita Āptya appears among the Persians split into two persons, two related heroes. The epithet of the ancient mythological being is here, as often, become an independent person. Kereshaspa appears as the son of Thrita who kills a frightful dragon. But a more celebrated dragon killer is the son of Āthwya, one of the greatest heroes of the Persian sagas. His name Thraetona Āthwyāna is a sort of double patronymic whose first form is doubtless clearly identical to Thrita

---

[178] *RV* VIII,41,6.

[179] *RV* I,105,9.

[180] *RV* I,158,5.

[181] There can be no doubt that the names āthwya and āptya are originally identical; there are just differences of opinion among scholars regarding the phonetic transformation, cf. Pischel, *Vedische Studien*, I,p.186; Bartholomae, *Arische Forschungen*, I, pp.8f; also *Indogermanische Forschungen*, I,pp.180f.

and is reminiscent of the Vedic Traitana, whereas the second is obviously derived from Āthwya. It therefore unites in this double name the derivations of those two names that the Vedic god Trita Āptya bears, and that confirms to us the supposition that the double name is old and the separation into two persons Thrita and Āthwya emerged later.

The much celebrated heroic deed of Thraetona Āthwyāna is the subjugation of the frightful serpent Azi Dahāka that corresponds to the dragon Ahi-Vrtra in the Veda. 'This is the deed on which the fame of Thraetona is based; it constitutes the central point of his story, it is his entire history.'[182] It is the same deed that is credited especially to Indra in the Veda, but also to Trita Āptya, as whose Zend Avestaic counterpart in this aspect now Thraetona Āthwyāna appears, along with a companion Kereshaspa by his side, who has accomplished a similar deed, whereas the figure of Indra, as is well-known, has disappeared almost without a trace from the mythic world of the Persians. Here the son accomplishes the deed that originally the father accomplished and that the mythological counterpart of the father, Trita Āptya, carries out in the Veda. In the Persian heroic sagas, Kereshaspa becomes the hero Gershasp and Thraetona the still more famous hero Feridun.

There is no doubt that we have here before us primordial myths of gods of lightning and thunderstorm that destroy the evil cloud demons, serpents or dragons – closely connected to Soma-Haoma, the heavenly Mead, that is also closely connected in India to Indra.

---

[182]    Cf. Roth in his fine essay, 'Die Sage von Feridun in Indien und Iran', *Zeitschrift der deutschen morgenländischen Gesellschaft*, vol.II, pp.218,219.

In a most remarkable way, however, the name of the Persian Thraetona Āthwyāna, who is quite doubtlessly closely related to the Indian Trita Āptya, recalls the name of the Greek goddess Athena, the daughter of the Triton – Tritonis Athana, Athene Tritogeneia. This surprising consonance already led the older comparative mythologists to identify the Persian hero and the Greek goddess and to explain the two, and also obviously the Indian Trita Āptya, as being originally related.[183] This relationship, however strange it may appear at first glance, however much stimulus it may have offered to modern linguistic scepticism, proves – the more thoroughly we examine the matter, the deeper we discover and understand the primordial roots in the nature of those three mythological figures – to be doubtlessly correct, indeed irrefutable. And if it was originally the remarkable consonance of the names that led significant scholars to relate Athene Tritogeneia, Tritonis Athena to Thraetona Āthwyāna and further to Trita Āptya, it is now rather the objective reasons – the original identity of nature that is becoming increasingly clearer – that make us adhere to that identification.

There can be no doubt that we have to recognize in Athene, according to her original character, a goddess of lightning and thunderstorm or – as Roscher formulates it – a goddess of storm clouds and lightning.[184] Proceeding further from this point

---

[183] One may compare the pioneering, even if in many details now outdated, essay of Theodor Benfey in the *Nachrichten von der königlichen Gesellschaft der Wissenschaften und der Georg-August Universität zu Göttingen*, 1868, pp.36-60: 'τρῑτωνιδ Ἀθάνα, Femininum des Zendischen Masculinum Thraetāna Athwyāna. Ein Beitrag zur vergleichenden Mythologie'.

[184] Cf. Roscher in his *Mythologisches Lexikon*, vol.I, pp.675f (see under 'Athene').

of departure the character of the superb goddess can be completely satisfyingly understood in all essential aspects, as Benfey and Roscher have already quite correctly recognized.[185] It is the same starting point that we have established for the Persian hero Feridun, Thraetona Āthwyāna – the same sphere in which the Indian Trita Āptya moves in a more primitive form. The female form in the case of Athena apparently comes on account of the particular Greek development.[186] In any case, the difference of gender should mislead us as little here as in the case of the solar deities where, for example, among the Latvians a male god, Uhsing, is the counterpart of the Indian Usha, in the Edda a female Sol that of the Latin Sol, etc.

As the warlike goddess of lightning and storm Pallas Athene is shown to us from the most ancient times in the typical accoutrements of shield and lance. There is no doubt that we have to recognize in the shield the dark storm clouds. That even is why she befits Zeus, the great storm god, who finds himself reborn in womanly form as it were and thus stands in closest relationship to her. The lance that the goddess flings is clearly enough the lightning – it is also in pictorial representation often replaced by a lightning bolt or bolts.[187] That is why Athena can also boast that she alone knows the entrance to the bower where the lighting is hidden.[188] The epithet Pallas designates Athena perhaps as the hurler of the

---

[185] Cf. Benfey, *op.cit.*, pp.56f., Roscher, *op.cit.*, p.687.

[186] Cf. Benfey, *op.cit.*, p.55.

[187] Cf. Preller, *op.cit.*, I, p.157; Roscher, *op.cit.*, p.677. Particularly Macedonian coins show the goddess swinging the lightning with the right hand and raising the shield with the left. Similarly in Athens, Syracuse, and on the coins of the Graeco-Indian kings.

[188] Cf. Preller, *op.cit.*, I, p.157; Roscher, *op.cit.*, p.677.

lance, or the goddess who hurls the lightning – and the hurled lance is also, accordingly, characteristic of the so-called Palladians[189] since the most ancient times.

Athena has her warlike nature in common with the other gods of lightning and storm of the Āryans, following the most ancient imagination of these peoples, who believed that they saw in storms the battle of a good god with evil spirits. Athena herself soon appears as a bold fighter and defeater of such evil spirits, especially of Gorgon[190] and the Giants,[191] soon she accompanies her chosen heroes defending and helping them – Herakles,[192] Perseus,[193] Bellerophon[194] – in such a battle. The warlike character of her nature allows Athena naturally to become, in general, a goddess of war,[195] just as the storm god Indra became the god of battle of the Vedic Indians.

But not only her battle but also her origin places Athena in the region of the heavenly clouds, in the drama of the storm. She belongs to the waters,

---

[189]  Cf. Preller, *op.cit.*, I, pp.156,157.

[190]  [The three Gorgon sisters, who included Medusa, were monstrous beings who had the power to turn people to stone.]

[191]  [The Giants were a tremendously powerful race born of Uranus and Gaia from the semen of Uranus when he was castrated by his Titan son Chronos. They were fought and defeated by the gods of Olympus in the so-called Gigantomachy.]

[192]  [Herakles was the son of Zeus and a mortal woman Alcmene. Zeus' consort Hera, in her jealousy of Alcmene, wished to prevent the birth of Herakles but the infant was protected and supported by Athena.]

[193]  [Perseus was another son of Zeus and Danaë, daughter of the King of Argos. Athena helped Perseus slay the Gorgon Medusa.]

[194]  [Bellerophon was the son of Poseidon and Eurynome who tamed the winged horse Pegasus (son of Poseidon and Medusa) with the help of Athena's magic bridle.]

[195]  Cf. Roscher, *op.cit.*, pp.678f; Preller, *op.cit.*, I, pp.175f.

she originates from them, and indeed, originally, doubtlessly from the waters of the heavenly clouds, as Bergk[196] has convincingly demonstrated. That is why she is called the daughter of the Triton, Tritonis, Tritogeneia, rising from Triton, the sea or river which the ancients sought in different places, and thought that they had finally found in the Triton Lake of Libya, whereas it was a question originally of the waters of the clouds.[197] But even the other, well-known saga of the birth of Athena from the head of Zeus is nothing but another form of the primordial myth of the birth of the lightning- and storm goddess from the clouds. The god of the heavens, Zeus, is supposed to have swallowed Metis, a daughter of Oceanus, impregnated by him, out of fear of the birth of a son and then borne Athena from his head. Hephaestos, or Prometheus, split his head with an axe for this purpose. But Athena springs forth with shining armour, with spear swung high, provided with a shield and letting out loud battle cries. These are clearly mythological images that are based on weather phenomena. The goddess of lightning and storm emerges amidst thunder and lightning from the heavenly clouds, which are understood here as the curly-haired head of the father of heaven, Zeus, that the fire god Hephaestos or Prometheus splits. The obvious significance is supported more definitely in another version of the saga according to which Athena was hidden in a cloud and, as a result of a lightning stroke from Zeus, suddenly emerged from the same.[198]

---

[196]  [Theodor Bergk (1812-1881) was a German philologist who specialized in classical Greek literature.]

[197]  Cf. Preller, *op.cit.*, I, p.152.

[198]  Cf. Roscher, *op.cit.*, p.676; also Preller, *op.cit.*, pp.154ff.

Nothing is more natural than that an ancient storm god is conceived in close relation to the flourishing of vegetation, agriculture and forestry as that emerges forcefully in the case of Athena in Attica. If Athena is also, to a certain extent, the goddess of spinning and weaving, this characteristic too has long been derived correctly from the nature of the storm goddess.[199] Clouds and mist emerge, according to a widespread idea, as a sort of ghost or cloth. The goddess operates in heaven, spins and weaves clouds and mists. If, finally, Athena is celebrated quite especially as the goddess of the illuminated intelligence, then Benfey must already have been right, who derives the goddess of wisdom from the goddess of lightning insofar as the lightning suddenly illuminates the darkness. The Greeks compared the lightning to an appropriate or exciting thought.[200] But we must also recall that the Vedic Trita is a wise god, as we have already seen – that all wisdom resides in him as the hub in the wheel.

But more important than all this for us, in the present case, is the fact that Athena is considered the inventor of the weapon dance and that she, according to the Orphic hymns, appears as the leader of the Curetes. She is supposed to have danced the Pyrrhic dance first after the victorious conclusion of the Gigantomachy, thus as a dance of peace and victory.[201] That was expressed also in the religion dedicated to her for, for the celebration of that great and famous victory, or for the honouring of Athena, the Pyrrhic dance was performed during the Panathenaea[202] with a specially

---

[199]   Cf. Roscher, *op.cit.*, p.681; Preller, *op.cit.*, I, pp.171,176,184.

[200]   Cf. Benfey, *op.cit.*, p.57; Roscher, *op.cit.*, p.687n.

[201]   Cf. Preller, *op.cit.*, I, p.62, n.6; Roscher, *op.cit.*, p.680.

[202]   [The Panathenaea was a festival that was held annually in

mimetic-orchestral setting.[203] Of course, in the victory over the Giants many gods had participated, but above all Zeus and Athena, as well as the great hero Hercules, whose assistance was a decisive one. Let us envision the nature of these gods and their opponents: Hercules corresponds naturally to Indra,[204] but Zeus is the great god of heaven and storm god who appropriated to himself the activity of the ancient storm giants. Athena is, as we know, related to the Indian Trita Āptya, the precursor and naturally related alter ego of Indra who also appears as his military comrade and assistant. But the giants are enormous, hulky enemies of the gods of prehistory and are, according to the evidence of monuments, spirits with snake feet, perhaps already since the most ancient times imagined as half men and half snakes or dragons.[205] In the gigantomachy

---

Athens in honour of Athena. It culminated in a hecatomb, or sacrifice of a hundred oxen.]

[203]   Cf. Preller, *op.cit.*, I, p.183.

[204]   It is impossible for us to establish this correspondence since that would lead us far away and the question is not of essential significance for the development indicated above. Individual deeds of Hercules have already for a long time been compared rightly to corresponding deeds of Indra. I give some thorough comparisons of both divine figures and evidence of their original identity in the second volume of my *Altarische Religion*.

[205]   It was believed earlier that the Giants were to be thought of only as humanly formed giants and that the snake-feet of these enemies of the gods was to be considered only an invention of the Hellenistic age (cf. Preller, *op.cit.* I, pp.61,62; Roscher, *Lexikon*, p.1670, see 'Giganten'); however, this view may now be considered as having been superseded. The Hellenistic age certainly did not invent the snake-feet of the Giants, rather this is based on much older mythological tradition that is expressed even in the art of the sixth century, whereas the human form is perhaps to be ascribed to epic influence. Cf., in this context, E. Kuhnert in Roscher's *Lexikon*, pp.1670-1673, see under 'Giganten'.

therefore it is essentially a question of a victory of those Greek gods that correspond to the Indian gods Indra and Trita, a victory over dangerous evil spirits that were at least partially imagined in serpentine form. This victory therefore corresponds essentially to one of the many victories that Indra effects over his daemonic opponents in the form of snakes. If Athena is supposed to have danced the Pyrrhic dance first after this victory, there appears before us therein the close relation between dragon victory and weapon dance that we had to surmise in the case of the religious drama in India and that we have encountered already also on Germanic soil. But we see ourselves approaching more closely the Indian religious drama if we may consider the relationship of Athena to the Curetes as ancient – as the Orphic hymns presents it to us – when Athena really acted, even if only temporarily and occasionally, as leader of the choir of the Curetes. For this relationship would – with the close relationship of Indra and Trita – correspond essentially to the relationship of Indra to the Maruts that we are already familiar with in the Vedic hymns. The dance of victory and peace of Athena and the Curetes or the dance of the Pyrrhicists during the Panathenaea, is comparable to the weapon dance that we have posited of the Maruts and of Indra after the victory over Ahi-Vrtra.

On the other hand, we are led in a quite different direction when we find the Curetes connected to Rhea, when they emerge occasionally also in the Dionysiac Thiasus,[206] when the Corybantes, their closest relatives, are grouped with Cybele and Dionysus. There we

---

[206]   [The thiasus of Dionysus was the procession of the ecstatic followers of the god. It included the female maenads, and other nature spirits such as sileni, satyrs and the god Pan.]

have the connection of the weapon dancing spirits with the gods of fertility corresponding entirely to the connection of the Maruts to their father Rudra-Shiva – who is originally identical to Dionysus – and corresponding also to the relation of our Germanic weapon dancers to Woden in the Giant dance of Yorkshire and to the many theriomorphic or even anthropomorphic spirits of vegetation or fertility that we must understand as primitive precursors of the great gods of fertility.

But we must now turn to the Romans!

Certainly Müllenhoff was right, as we saw, when he compared the Roman Salii, the warlike armed dancers of Mars, to the Germanic weapon dancers and placed even the strange form of Mamurius Veturius connected to them – alongside the similarly strange forms that appear on Germanic soil – with the weapon dancers. But equally rightly did the ancients compare the Salii with the Curetes, even though the latter are spirit dancers whereas the Salii represent a priestly college. We must therefore consider more closely the Salii and the god Mars who is closely connected to them.

The Salii of Mars were a very respected college of twelve excellent priestly dancers who performed their dance in Rome in the month of March sacred to their god. They had a leader, the so-called *magister*,[207] a principal dancer, and perhaps also a principal singer. They were armed in a warlike manner with the sacred shield of Mars, the so-called *ancilia*,[208] in their left hand, with their sword on the side, and a small lance in their

---

[207]   [master]

[208]   [The ancilia was the sacred shield that fell from the heavens during the reign of Numa Pompilius. It was kept in the Temple of Mars.]

right hand. On their head they wore the *apex*,[209] the priestly headdress that took the form of a helmet in their case. In their ancient hymns they invoked the state gods of the Romans but also sang of the most famous heroes of the earliest times and of their deeds. At their end of their song they used to invoke Mamurius Veturius, that mythological smith, who is supposed to have manufactured, on Numa's wish, in addition to a shield fallen from the heavens, the remaining eleven.[210] It seemed to accord badly with this service, and with the reverence accorded to him when, on the day before the Ides of March, a man whom they called Mamurius Veturius clothed in skins was led through the city flogged out of the city with long white sticks. However, it was also proven clearly long ago that this old smith was originally none other than the spirit of vegetation and fertility who had grown old who had to be driven out annually or replaced by a new, as it were rejuvenated, one. One can, along with Usener, call him the god of the old year, which rather comes to the same thing. Preller already, quite correctly, made the comparison of the customs of the Germanic peoples and the Slavs who drive out the winter, or death, in mimetic representations, in spring – often precisely in March – and Usener established it more firmly and deeply in their connection to the Roman custom.[211] The name of Mamurius is doubtless connected clearly to the name of Mars, the epithet Veturius designates him as the old Mars of the past year. He is the spirit

---

[209]    [The apex was a hat worn by the Salian priests and Flamines.]

[210]    [See Plutarch, *Life of Numa*, 13.]

[211]    Cf. Preller, *Römische Mythologie*, 3rd ed., I , p.360; Usener in the *Rheinisches Museum für Philologie*, vol.30, pp.213f; Roscher, *Lexikon*, p.2419, see under 'Mars'.

of vegetation that has grown old, the old Mars of the past year, who is revered by the Salii but also driven out by the same,[212] while it was believed that a new young Mars was born on 1 March. It is nothing but that typical renewal that we have spoken of many times already. I need only briefly recall the death and resurrection of Dionysus, the apparently dead but reawakening man in the Shiva festival, the Yuletide ram that is shot but lives again, Schnortison, and all the related figures and customs. In the Roman custom, as also often elsewhere, the expulsion stands for death. It is understood in this manner just as easily as the preceding veneration of the old man. But the Salii are the worshippers of the old and the young Mars. Their dances originating from the earliest times – as the comparison demonstrates – promote and celebrate at the same time the victory of the new year, of spring, of the god of fertility who has been reborn.

1 March was considered the birthday of Mars. Then the Salii brought forth their shields in order to perform their weapon dance with them. Involuntarily we are reminded here of the Corybantes, who similarly dance around the child Zeus,[213] as also the Giant dancers of Yorkshire who swing two swords around the neck of a boy without hurting him, a boy whom we have identified as the young spirit of fertility. On 9 March, there took place a repeated festival celebration on the part of the Salii. On 14 March, they drove out Mamurius

---

[212]    Cf. Roscher, *Lexikon*, p.2400, see under 'Mars'.

[213]    'This Cretan Zeus stood closer to the Dionysus of the mysteries than to the Olympian Zeus of the normal Greek religious belief' remarks even Preller quite accurately (*Griechische Mythologie*, I, p.527). One recalls, quite apart from the story of his birth, the grave of Zeus that was indicated in Crete. What sense would that have had for the great god of the heavens?

Veturius in the manner already stated and, on that same day, there took place, in honour of Mars, the so-called Equirria, a race on the Campus Martius. In the celebration of 17 March, the Quirinalian Salii[214] took part – another college of priestly dancers who were especially consecrated to Quirinus, the Sabine Mars, who had likewise found, as is well-known, a firm place of worship in Rome. The Salii of Mars, in contrast to the latter, were called the Palatinate, since they had their curia[215] on the Palatine Hill. They appeared, dancing and sacrificing, again on 19 March in the presence of the Pontifex and the Tribunus Celerum.[216] They had an important procession also on 23 March, the day of the so-called Tubilustrium.[217] Finally, these March festivities came to a close on the 24th of the month.[218]

Ever since the association with the Sabines,[219] Rome possessed, alongside the Salii of Mars, also that other Salii college that was just mentioned. But also in Tibur there was one such that was dedicated to the service of Hercules, the Greek Herakles, who is originally related to Indra. Here therefore the Salii appeared in connection with the great victor over the dragon and

---

[214]   [The Salian Collini priests associated with the Quirinalian college; see above p.26.]

[215]   [government]

[216]   [the commander of the cavalry]

[217]   Cf. Roscher, *Lexikon*, pp 2401,2402; Preller, *Römische Mythologie*, 3rd ed., I, pp.363 364.

[218]   Cf. Roscher, *Lexikon*, pp.2399-2403; Preller, *Römische Mythologie*, 3rd ed., I, pp.346, 355-366 .

[219]   [The Sabines were an Italic people who inhabited the cenral Apennine mountains. Most of the Sabines were absorbed into Rome after the foundation of Rome in the early 8th century B.C. and the others were incorporated into the Roman Republic from the 6th century B.C. on.]

other monsters, as we see the Maruts connected with Indra in India, in England the sword dancers with Snapdragon or St. George. That is to be noted well even if we may not speak of Hercules as a genuine ancient Roman god. The connection is important whether it was developed on Italian soil or originated from Greece. But there were also otherwise, 'sodalities of Salii since time immemorial'[220] in many cities of Italy. The institution of priestly dancers is clearly seen to be a very ancient one rooted firmly in Italian soil. But the Salii are most closely connected to Mars. Indeed, Preller is right when he says that Mars himself was doublessly thought of as a Salian.[221]

But Mars is, doubtlessly clearly, especially a great god of fertility, of the procreative life-force, as Preller already recognized and presented quite correctly. On the other hand, it signifies a regression in scholarship when Wissowa wishes to stamp Mars again as a mere god of war. He is certainly a war god, but he is not that in the first place and one who thinks that he understands his nature thus is certainly misled. The nature of Mars is revealed very clearly in the ancient venerable cult of the Fratres Arvales[222] in the meadow of Dea Dia,[223] the solemn goddess of the field of the Roman city. Here Mars is invoked as the principal god in the ancient hymn of the farmers along with the Lares and the Semones, that is, with the departed souls of the ancestors and the gods of sowing. It is

---

[220]    Cf. Preller, *op.cit.*, I, p.347.

[221]    Cf. Preller, *ibid.*, pp.347,348.

[222]    [The *fratres arvales* were priests of the goddess of fertility Dea Dia.]

[223]    [Dea Dia was a Roman goddess of fertility identified with Ceres and the Greek Demeter.]

the same characteristic connection of death cult and agrarian cult that emerges clearly enough many times even otherwise in Rome. Mars is the leader of souls and god of fertility at the same time, just as Wotan-Odin, Dionysus-Hermes and Rudra-Shiva are, as whose closest relative he appears on Italian soil. The orgiasm in which we see him rushing and jumping in the Arval hymn[224] is the vegetation orgiasm of the Dionysiac troops that we have long been familiar with, of the Perchten jumpers and all the many related phenomena – it has nothing to do with warlike fury. The whip that he seems to wield corresponds to the life-awakening rod in the hand of so many vegetation spirits, of the Corn Wolf, the Corn Cat, the May King, Pelzmärtel, Farmhand Rupert,[225] etc.;[226] it corresponds likewise to the thongs[227] with which the Luperci, 'the wolf cubs,'[228] accost women and girls, awakening fertility during the Lupercalia festivities, it corresponds perhaps most closely to the thongs or switches with which the Salii

---

[224] The text of the old religious hymn may be translated rather in the following manner: 'Help us, you Lares! Let no plague come over the people, O Mars! Be appeased, wild Mars, jump over the threshold! Stop, scourge! Invoke all the gods of sowing, one by one, here! Help us, Mars! Triumph! Triumph!

[225] [Knecht Ruprecht is the manservant companion of St. Nikolaus and is characterized by his dark clothes and visage, probably due to his climb through the chimney.]

[226] Cf. Mannhardt, *Wald- und Feldkulte*, I, p.365; II, pp ;173,187,326,343. In Kadań, in the Saaz district of Bohemia, they say that the Corn Mother bears a whip in her hand, cf. Mannhardt, *Mythologische Forschungen*, p.303.

[227] [The thongs were cut from the skins of the animals – normally goats and a dog – that were sacrificed.]

[228] [The Luperci were the priests who officiated annually at the Lupercalia festivities on February 15.]

strike.[229] This too is a vegetation or fertility magic.

It is not the war god but the great god of fertility Mars whom we see ruling in the field of the field goddess in the hymn of the farmers. It is also him to whom the Roman farmer prays during the consecration of the field, the Ambarvalia.[230] He also emerges clearly in the very characteristic figure of Mars Silvanus, as well as in the close relationship of the great god to the fauns and sylphs, the spirits of vegetation and fertility of Roman religion that correspond so clearly, and are originally related, to the Greek satyrs and sileni,[231] pans and paniskoi,[232] our wild people, wood people, Schratten[233] and Fänggen,[234] etc. Mars is the great god of this circle who rises far above it but belongs to it in his roots. The relationship of Mars to departed souls was in all probability originally stronger and closer than we perceive and the reason for this weakening can perhaps be guessed. According to the ancient Āryan belief souls did not in any way dwell solely, or predominantly, in the depths of the earth. They travelled in wind and storm through the air, they dwelt in mountains, woods and the water, and continued their life also in animals and plants. But in the Roman belief the latter ideas are no longer very noticeable. The dark core of the earth

---

[229] Cf. the 'pellem virgis ferire' of the Salii, Roscher's Lexikon, p.2409, see under 'Mars'.

[230] [Ambarvalia was a Roman agricultural fertility rite that involved the sacrifice of a bull, a sow and a sheep.]

[231] [Ithyphallic satyrs and sileni are part of the Dionysiac retinue; see above p. 97n]

[232] [Paniskoi are Pan-like creatures who formed part of the Dionysiac thiasus.]

[233] [Schratten are spirits personifying the moss attached to trees.]

[234] [The Fänggen are female wood spirits in western Austrian folklore.]

is considered the dwelling place of departed souls. But Mars is not a chthonic god and therefore we see that in this development his relationship to the realm of spirits had to weaken. Still, the latter is still recognizable in many regards. Beans are sacred to Mars[235] and we recognize beans as specific soul offerings in the funerary cult. Indeed, beans had this significance even in the earliest Āryan times.[236] But especially important is the already mentioned relationship of Mars with the Lares in the cult of the fratres arvales. For, the Lares are, already according to the completely correct view of the ancients, departed souls of the ancestors, and indeed souls of good men,[237] in contrast to the Lares and Lemures, the restless spectral spirits and ghosts of the evil, the wicked. The *lares* were worshipped at home alongside Vesta and the Penates;[238] they were worshipped also at crossroads, a very characteristic place for departed souls. It was these *lares compitales*[239] and *viales*[240] that were also considered as benevolent gods of the fields producing fertility and were invoked in this sense – the typical development of souls into spirits of fertility. One imagined and figured the *lares* as having Dionysiac attributes, dancing, with cup

---

[235] Cf. Roscher, *Lexikon*, p.2429, see under 'Mars'.

[236] Cf. my proofs regarding this point in the *Wiener Zeitschrift für die Kunde des Morgenlandes*, vol.XV, pp.187-212.

[237] Cf. Preller, *Römische Mythologie*, 3rd ed., II, p.103 ; H. Ehrlich, *Zeitschrift für vergleichende Sprachforschung*, vol.41, pp.295-304.

[238] [The Di Penates were domestic deities, though they also had a dignified public position as gods related to Vesta, guardian of the home and the nation.]

[239] [The lares compitales were deities presiding over cossroads. Lares were guardian spirits developed from earlier hero ancestors who presided over homes and public institutions.]

[240] [The lares viales were deities presiding over roads.]

and drinking horn in their hands, pouring out wine and joyously excited.[241] Whether this conception may have originated in Greece or – at least partially – had native Italian roots, in any case, it agrees best with the conception of the Dionysiac procession as a form of army of souls. However, other, genuine Roman, phenomenal forms of the Lares were also known. They were also imagined as armed in a warlike manner as *lares militares*. And we see such figured on coins, spear in hand, clothed in skins around the hips, a dog at their feet.[242] These *lares* armed in a warlike manner agree, in their appearance, naturally best with Mars, whom we could imagine as the leader of a troop of such *lares*. Nigidius Figulus may also have thought of them when he compared the Curetes with the *lares*. But in a more immediate way does the image of the Salii, the warlike armed dancers of Mars, come to mind.

If Corybantes and Curetes were represented in the religion by dancing priests armed in a warlike manner, if we must presume the same for the Maruts, if it is, accordingly, obvious to look for the mythological prototype of the Germanic sword dancers in the army of souls armed in a warlike manner, the Einherjar, the *animae militum interfectorum*, the raging army, then, in view of the dancing troop of Salii, the question naturally arises – Do not even these priestly dancers represent in a cultic mimetic way the army of souls armed in a warlike manner that must be naturally closer to Mars than souls conceived in other ways?

---

[241]  Cf. Roscher, *Lexikon*, pp.1891f, see under 'Lares'; Preller, *op.cit.*, II, p.109, n.1.

[242]  Cf. Roscher, *op.cit.*, p.1872, see under 'Lares'; H. Ehrlich, *op.cit.*, p.298.

I think we must answer this question affirmatively even if no *lares militares*[243] are evident to us on Roman monuments. It is, however, no longer doubtful that the weapon dance originates in the earliest Āryan times and only for that period must we definitely claim this mythological idea as a basis. However, even the *lares militares* show us now that a similar idea was in no way alien to the Romans, that it had maintained itself vividly even if not in a predominant way. Alongside the joyous Dionysiac *lares* we have here also the ones armed in a warlike manner and the Salii are – we may assume – basically the earthly reflection represented by priests of a troop of *lares* armed in a warlike manner similar, even if not identical, to those whose image we see on coins – similar to the troop of Maruts and the dancing chorus of Curetes. And if Mars himself has been rightly called a Salian, he may perhaps with greater justification be called a *lar militaris* who developed into a great god, the former ancient leader of the souls armed in a warlike manner, just as Odin is the leader of the Einherjar.

And precisely with this precondition is best understood the development of Mars into the great war god of the Romans. He possessed a warlike character naturally in himself. He was a great god of souls and fertility but he was also always a powerful armed warrior and leader of a corresponding troop of warriors. This development, that is in itself understandable, is also not isolated. It finds a clear parallel in the north. Even Odin became a great god of war in Scandinavia; but therein it is not less true that he is naturally the great leader of souls and the god of fertility.

If Mars with his Salii is thus approximated in a surprising way to the Maruts, then another element

---

[243]    [Military lares]

deserves to be highlighted that was noted and discussed much earlier but was not in itself capable of proving the connection of these mythological figures in a convincing manner but can now serve as a further powerful support for our comparison. I mean the similarity of the names. Already Adalbert Kuhn compared Mars and the Maruts with inspired insight and maintained the identity of these names.[244] After him, Bradke investigated the linguistic question thoroughly and finely and, in my opinion, provided the conclusive evidence that the names in fact go together and that their identification may be considered as well-grounded.[245] Of course the etymology of the names is not clear, their roots are still questionable,[246] but their identity can be maintained, and it is for us of the greatest significance, for it supports emphatically the connection of the Italian Mars with the Maruts and their father Rudra that has been obtained by us by other means.

The establishment of this connection, however, brings for us, in the case of Mars, a further gain. It is clear that the ancient gods and spirits of souls and fertility of the Āryans mostly – even if not always – exhibit a close relationship to the wind and often are precisely wind gods and spirits. This corresponds to the most ancient of the conduct of souls through air and wind. For that great group of beings that correspond to the Roman silvans and fauns Mannhardt has, as the

---

[244] Cf. Kuhn, *Zeitschrift für deutsches Altertum*, vol.V, pp;488f. Of course Kuhn's interpretations are in some details no longer tenable, but he was the first to have the inspired intuition.

[245] Cf. P. v. Bradke, *Zeitschrift der deutschen morgenländischen Gesellschaft*, vol.40, pp.349-361.

[246] For my part I consider it now likely that the root 'mar', to gleam, to shine, is at the basis of the name.

definite result of his deep and thorough researches, presented such a relationship to the wind and the expression of their life in the wind. The Roman figures, however; do not exhibit this connection and even in the case of Mars, the great god of this circle, no clear connection with wind and storm is perceptible. It is obvious to surmise that it lost it because, in the Roman belief, the souls do not travel in wind and storm but dwell in the depths of the earth. However, a positive indication would be desirable and such is offered, I think, by the identity of Mars and Marut. For, there is no doubt that the Maruts are storm gods. That allows us to conclude with greater certainty than before even in the case of Mars an ancient relationship to wind and storm.[247] If he lost this relationship in the course of time, he still belongs originally to that important group of primordial gods of wind, souls and fertility, as whose greatest representative we recognize Wotan-Odin, Dionysus-Hermes, Rudra-Shiva.

The circle is now closed that connects the Marut troop of weapon dancers with the Germanic sword dancers, the Greek Curetes, the Phrygian Corybantes, the Roman Salii and we may venture to sketch in outline those mythological ideas and religious customs of the earliest Āryan times that underlie all of them.

Among the different forms in which the Āryans of the earliest times conceived of the army of departed

---

[247]   Apart from Kuhn and Bradke, Graβmann (*Zeitschrift für vergleichende Sprachforschung*, 16, p.162) and Leo Meyer (*Zur ältesten Geschichte der griechischen Mythologie*, p.47) have supported the identification of Mars=Marut, or the stormy nature of Mars. It is very understandable that this view met with resistance (cf. Roscher's *Lexikon*, p.2436, see under 'Mars'; Jordan's note in Preller, *op.cit.*, I, p.334); however, now, one can no longer discount this easily. As we have seen, it possesses the greatest verisimilitude.

souls is, as one of the most important, also the idea of a troop armed young warriors. One thought of these as dancing and performing a weapon dance but also faring through the air in wind and storm – the raging army, the Maruts. Both especially, or even exclusively, in certain seasons of the year, in the major segments of the natural division of time. Especially perhaps at the beginning of spring, but also at the beginning of autumn and in midwinter, the Germanic Yuletide. The weapon dance of these youths had a double beneficial effect: protecting from injury and disease, illnesses of all sorts, stimulating and promoting growth and fertility in the entire sphere of natural life. For this reason one naturally imagined these mythological weapon dancers as closely related to major and minor gods and spirits of fertility. Not only with those great divine figures as whose representatives and heirs we recognize Wotan-Odin among the Germanic peoples, Rudra-Shiva and his wife among the Indians, Dionysus and Rhea-Cybele, among the Romans Mars, but also with much more ancient theriomorphic or otherwise strangely imagined spirits of vegetation that survive in the English Tommy and Bessy, in Schnortison and the Fool of the Germanic sword dancers, in the satyrs and sileni of the Greeks, in the Mamurius Veturius of the Roman Salii, etc. One perhaps imagined them also as dancing around and protecting a boy child with their weapons – the new-born god of vegetation and fertility: the child Dionysus among the Corybantes, the Zeus child among the Curetes, the boy around whose head two swords are swung in the Giants dance in Yorkshire; and the same image perhaps stood originally also in the background of the Salii dance that began on the birthday of the god Mars and continued through the month of his birth.

But one imagined these youthful weapon dancers equally naturally also in connection with the strong, warlike divinities of lightning and storm who repeatedly help light and life to victory through powerful battles, kill evil demons and dragons and liberate the sun and the waters. We recognize them again in the Indra and Trita Āptya of the Indians, in Athena and Herakles-Hercules among the Greeks, in the Donner-Thor of the Germans. And for this reason we see in India the Maruts associated with Indra and also with Trita Āptya, the Curetes in Greece with Athena, the Salii in Tibur with Hercules, the English sword dancers with the Snapdragon or St. George, the Christian representative of the mythological dragon-killer. We see them helping Indra in battle and see them celebrating with him and the related mythological figures the great victory in joyously spirited dances.

But they did not satisfy themselves with the play of ideas. They presented these images of the mythological fancy also vividly in a mimetic manner, in the religious drama, with dance and song. And one attributed to such mimetic representation a magical-religious effect – an effect quite analogous to the power of those mythological beings, warding off evil, stimulating and promoting growth and fertility. It was this that lent to such a custom its great significance and importance, that gave it something like a higher, secret consecration. That maintained it alive, that allowed the Āryans to hold on tenaciously and stubbornly to such a custom for centuries, even millennia, even in times and circumstances that were alien and hostile to it through the rule of a quite different religion. It was not an idle game, a mere entertainment that could be substituted by other entertainments. One thought rather that one effected something important through such a drama. Thus it could not be given up and maintained itself in strenuous practice – for example, among the Germanic peoples – even when the original sense and goal of the custom was long forgotten and could hardly be divined even dimly. One only knew still that the ancestors had continuously practiced and revered it – and so one practiced it further and was glad to do so for, along with its deep significance, it also offered a genuine folklorish entertainment.

Certainly there must have been many variations of the drama already in the earliest Āryan times even if the weapon dance always remained the most important, the core and climax. We can easily reconstruct such variations from the extant remnants of the custom. There the great heroic deeds of the divine dragon killer were extolled, as the Maruts extol the deeds of Indra, there dances and songs were offered in his honour and he himself danced his victory dance, as Indra and St. George dance, as perhaps also the Greeks in the misty prehistory saw their Athena dancing. There they danced around the newborn god of fertility, as the Corybantes danced around the child Dionysus, the Curetes around the child Zeus-Dionysus, there one swung their swords above the head of the boy who represented this god, like the Giant dancers in Yorkshire. There the dancers sang about the deeds of the gods and the heroes of prehistory, there they invoked and praised also the ancient vegetation god of the past year, who offers to them so many gifts, but finally drive him out with blows, as the Salii invoke Mamurius Veturius and then finally beat him out of the city. There the spirit that has grown old is killed, like the Bessy of the English sword dancers, killed but to immediately be resurrected and dance again, like Schnortison in the swordfighter drama in Clausthal. There perhaps, already quite early on, seriousness and frivolity were mixed up. The original costume of the old spirit of vegetation gave sufficient occasion for the latter and not least the violence that was enacted against him when he was driven out, beaten or killed and allowed to live again and dance. But the weapon dance itself was certainly a serious matter. Not only because a religious aura, a sort of higher sanctity surrounded it but also certainly because in itself it was a serious, difficult performance, in no way free of danger. Of the bravery, strength and skill that the Germanic sword dancers displayed and to what height they at least often were able to raise the art of their warlike exercice one obtains a deep, lasting impression from many of the descriptions compiled by Müllenhoff. Already Tacitus admired unreservedly the weapon dance of the Germanic youths. Admiration is attested also in many other later descriptions of the sword dance in Ditmarschen and Hessen as well as on English soil. What prehistory contributed to it we do not know but it was certainly a serious and difficult exercise.

But even the drama connected with the dance may have been formed seriously and in a dignified manner even in such a way that it was able to exert a deep dramatic effect. Our Vedic dialogue hymns offer the most striking examples of this. Here the poet has shaped a singularly difficult conflict between Indra and the Maruts into an impressive drama into which, skillfully and genuinely dramatically, even the wise Agastya is drawn, which brings alive before our eyes Indra's powerful passion, his pride and his glory and yet finally fades away in a harmonious manner. The value of this small Vedic mystery is certainly the individual merit of its poet. But that one added a drama to the weapon dance – at least different dramatic actions and songs – was doubtless already an ancient practice. It was not definitely necessary, not indispensable, but certainly watched with interest already early on. We have already mentioned some typical actions of this sort – the best known is the driving out of Mamurius Veturius by the Salii. In Germanic lands we see often formally small dramas connected with the sword dance. We find examples of these in Müllenhoff and Mayer. And it is also not inconceivable that where the sword dancers appeared in connection with the dragon killer occasionally also the drama of the dragon killer preceded, although we do not have any direct evidence for it. In the pertinent mysteries of the Indians and the Germanic peoples at hand the stabbing of the dragon is always presumed as having happened earlier and extolled partly by the hero himself, partly by others. But even the stabbing of the dragon seems to have been alive as an ancient popular spring festival in German lands since the earliest times and has been preserved up to the present in many places and acquired local accretions. Germany and Austria, England, even France know such popular dramas in which as a rule the dragon killer frees a maiden from the violence of the dragon.[248] It would perhaps be worth the trouble

---

[248]  Cf., on this, Ernst Krause, *Die Trojaburgen Nordeuropas*, Glogau, 1893, pp.85-87. 'The dragon is conducted in great splendour through the city, then the battle play is performed in places with alternating speeches, then the dragon is stabbed, the king's daughter freed and the festival concluded with dances and plays. In France, many saints appear as dragon killers, in England, it is now mostly St. George (or Robin Hood, earlier Sir Bevis) of Snapdragon, who frees the May Queen; in Germany, there appear, along with St. George

to pursue this question and to trace the connection between such dramas and the weapon dance. It is in no way impossible that the stabbing of the dragon, even if represented in a still primitive form – one may and Siegfried, for example, in Wurmlingen near Tübingen, the counts of Wurmbrand as dragon killers of the popular sagas.' There follows an example:

'In the border town Furth in the Oberpflaz', narrates (Friedrich) Panzer, 'the 'stabbing of the dragon' is celebrated annually on the Sunday after Corpus Christi.' A king's daughter with a golden crown, her 'lady-in-waiting', a knight in armour on foot and a dragon made of wood moved from the inside by two men are the characters of the play. She sits on the 'hard stone' and narrates her distress to the knight, who consoles her and stabs, or kills, the monster as soon as it tries to catch her. Then she promises him, on behalf of her father, half of the kingdom. After twelve or fifteen hours, Bohemians and people from the Pfalz appear and take up in cloths the dragon blood that is spilt on the fields of flax, where it promotes growth and acts against witches. The Bohemians used to say that the dragon was the 'lindworm' (a Germanic dragon that lives in the forests) and the rescuer "Siegfried".

This information seems to me especially important and noteworthy on account of the use of the dragon blood made by the people. That points to a very ancient primitive religious custom. Krause cites also the 'dragon play' from the Middle Ages and the "*ludus draconis*" which, according to a document in Magdeburg in 1416, was henceforth forbidden to students. He comes to the conclusion that the dragon fight was 'the ancient play of the Germanic peoples and their neighbours from which not only the beginnings of dramatic art but also the knightly plays, the sword dances and the great festive round dances were developed which are, in the southern Slavic countries, still danced today in great festivity on the day of St. George, that is, of the Christianised Siegfried. Just as in antiquity, the dramatic plays and dances are connected to the killing of the Minotaur by Theseus, to the freeing of Ariadne and her dedication to Dionysus, just as the labyrinth ride of the Trojan play in Rome is supposed to have been instituted in honour of the spring goddess Frutis, our Whitsun jousting competition in Mainz and the riding around the Maypole too appear as inseparable from the festival of the May Queen as the Morris dance of the English in which a dragon, a dragon killer and a maiden acted as characters.'

remember the Cora,[249] in which a girdle represents the dragon of the dawn – was already a religious drama of the earliest Āryan times. However, we wish here to stop with the results that we have with certainty for that time – the magical religious weapon dance that was associated with songs and dramatic actions as well as the alternating association of the weapon dancers, on the one hand, with the dragon killer, the storm god or storm giants and, on the other, with the gods and spirits of fertility whereby the spirit of the year that has grown old is driven out or killed and the newborn god is danced around and protected with bare weapons.

---

In any case, an important suggestion lies before us – as the Krause book is generally very rich in interesting suggestions, in spite of its undeniable weakness in all linguistic matters – It is in no way unlikely that precisely the dragon fight was a religious mystery of the earliest Āryan times.

[249] [The Cora Indians are an indigenous tribe of northwestern Mexico.]

# OTHER BOOKS BY
# ALEXANDER JACOB

## THE GRAIL – TWO STUDIES

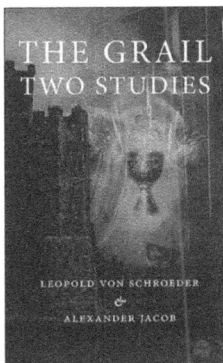

A proper understanding of the significance of the cultic object called the Holy Grail has eluded most scholars who have confined their research to western European literary and cultural sources, especially since the originally Celtic story of the Holy Grail underwent numerous bewildering metamorphoses in the romances of the Middle Ages. It was the Indologist Leopold von Schroeder's reading of the Grail story (1910) in the light of his knowledge of Indic mythology that first achieved a dramatic expansion of the field of Holy Grail scholarship. The only other scholar who developed a comprehensive comparative mythological study of the

Grail was perhaps Julius Evola in his Il *Mistero del Graal e la Tradizione Ghibellina dell'Impero* (1937).

Schroeder's fascinating elucidation of some of the key symbols of the Grail legends using his knowledge of ancient Indian literature is amplified by Alexander Jacob's reconstruction of the cosmological basis of these symbols and his analysis of the solar rituals that characterized the diverse yet related religions of the ancient Indo-Europeans.

# INDO-EUROPEAN MYTHOLOGY AND RELIGION: ESSAYS

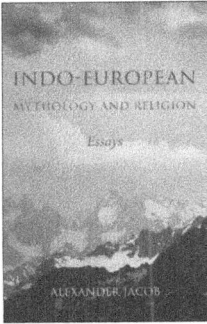

The essays presented in this collection are based on Alexander Jacob's earlier works, *Ātman: A Reconstruction of the Solar Cosmology of the Indo-Europeans*, Hildesheim: Georg Olms, 2005 and *Brahman: A Study of the Solar Rituals of the Indo-Europeans*, Hildesheim: Georg Olms, 2012. They expand on the cosmological and religious themes discussed in these books with special reference to the origins and development of the Indic and European spiritual traditions. Those familiar with the earlier works will not be surprised that Dr. Jacob's view of the term 'Indo-European' is rather more comprehensive than the more restricted term 'Āryan' that has hitherto been widely used as a synonym of it. And those interested in the Āryan ethos itself – chiefly on account of the German use of the term during the last war – may be surprised to learn that it does not consist in nationalistic virtues so much as in spiritual discipline and development – and that this development is characteristic of the religions of very extended and diversified branches of the Indo-European family.

VEDANTA, PLATO, AND KANT
BY PAUL DEUSSEN
TRANSLATED BY ALEXANDER JACOB

"The Kantian worldview, which always underlay all religion, philosophy, and art, could not have been the eternal truth if it did not emerge more or less clearly everywhere that the human mind penetrated into the depths, as this occurred, for example, in India through the Upanishads of the Vedas and the Vedanta based on them and in Greece through Parmenides and Plato. To consider both these phenomena in the light of the Kantian philosophy is the task that we have set ourselves here." - *Paul Deussen*

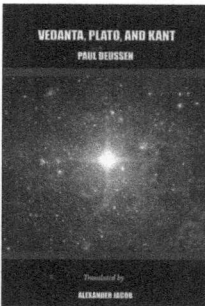

*Vedanta, Plato, and Kant* is a new translation. The book presents a defense of Shankara's Advaita Vedānta philosophy as well as an elucidation of the Greek Idealistic doctrines of Parmenides and Plato. In all these schools of thought, Deussen detects a similar basic understanding of the world as a mere appearance distinct from Ideal Reality. He approximated this understanding to the Kantian notion of 'things in themselves' (Dinge-an-sich) and noted a degeneration of the original Vedic and Upanishadic worldview in the philosophies that followed, such as the Sāmkhya and Buddhism, just as there was a corruption of Parmenides' doctrine of Being in the philosophy of his pupil Zeno. Similarly, he believes that Kant's revolutionary Idealistic insights in Germany were also distorted by the post-Kantian thinkers and not generally understood in their original form except by Arthur Schopenhauer (1788-1860), who developed the doctrine of the world as a mere representation produced by the innate intuitive forms within the Intellect – Space, Time, and Causality.

Includes a preface by Alexander Jacob (Translator).

## AGNI-VĀYU-ĀDITYA:
## THE INDO-EUROPEAN TRINITY OF FIRE

This abrégé of Jacob's 2005 study *Ātman: A Reconstruction of the Solar Cosmology of the Indo-Europeans* (Hildesheim: Georg Olms) focuses on the cosmological insights that inform ancient Indo-European religions and, in particular, on the most significant trinity worshipped by the ancient Indo-Āryans – Agni-Vāyu-Āditya – which represents the forms that the cosmic fire takes in the underworld of Earth before it is installed as the sun in the Heaven of our universe. This is not a sociological Trinity, as Dumézil's studies, for example, would lead one to believe. Rather, it is an understanding of the divine fire that informs the macrocosm as well as the human microcosm.

The present essay should thus serve to correct the misleading sociological orientations of Dumézilian comparative mythology. At the same time, it will give the reader a glimpse into the extraordinary depth of vision of the prisca theologia of the Indo-Europeans.

## NĀLEVARNAM:

## OF THE FOUR COMMUNITIES OR CASTES

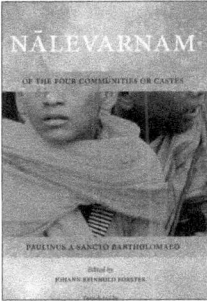

Paulinus a Sancto Bartholomaeo (1748-1806) was an Austrian Carmelite missionary – of Croatian origin – who worked in India and published a *Systema Brahmanicum liturgicum mythologicum civile* (*The Brāhmanical Liturgical, Mythological and Civil System*) in 1791 which was edited and translated into German in 1797 as *Darstellung der brahmanisch-indischen Götterlehre, religionsgebräuche und bürgerlichen Verfassung* (*An Account of the Brāhmanical Indian Mythology, Religious Customs and Civil Constitution*) by the naturalist Johann Reinhold Forster (1729-1798). The present translation of four chapters from this work dealing with the four main castes of India makes available to the English-speaking reader one of the earliest European accounts of the caste system as it existed in India at the end of the eighteenth century.